Margaret

The Angelical Conjunction

The Angelical

Patricia A. Watson

Conjunction

The Preacher-Physicians of Colonial New England

The University of Tennessee Press / Knoxville

Copyright © 1991 by
The University of Tennessee Press / Knoxville
All Rights Reserved.
Manufactured in the United States of America.
First Edition.

The paper in this book meets the minimum
requirements of the American National Standard
for Permanence of Paper for Printed Library
Materials. ☉   The binding materials have been chosen
for strength and durability.

Library of Congress Cataloging-in-Publication Data

Watson, Patricia A., 1956–
    The angelical conjunction : the preacher-physicians of colonial
New England / Patricia A. Watson.–1st ed.
       p. cm.
    Includes bibliographical references and index.
    ISBN 0-87049-696-4 (cloth: alk. paper)
    1. Clergy–New England–History. 2. Medicine–Religious
aspects–Christianity–History. 3. Physicians–New England–
Religious life. 4. Medicine–New England–History. I. Title.
BR530.W37 1991
277.4'07–dc20   90-22214
                                                            CIP

For JPG and JPS

Contents

Tables

Acknowledgments

I am particularly indebted to my former advisor at Johns Hopkins University, Jack P. Greene, who has provided me with much-needed support throughout the writing of this book. I also thank Gert H. Brieger and Jerome Bylebyl of the Institute of the History of Medicine, Johns Hopkins University School of Medicine, for their insightful criticism. J. Worth Estes generously and patiently read drafts of this study, offering sound comments and friendly advice. Harold Y. Vanderpool, Darrel W. Amundsen, and Ronald Numbers all helped steer me through the literature on religion and medicine and provided helpful criticism and references. Jon R. Polansky has given me encouragement and guidance since I began graduate school. I also am grateful to the members of Professor Greene's seminar in the history of Anglo-American colonization, who read and criticized many drafts of this work while I was a graduate student. Johns Hopkins University, the John Carter Brown Library, and the American Antiquarian Society provided funding for portions of the research for this study, and I am grateful. I thank the staff of the latter two institutions for pointing me towards valuable resources that otherwise I would have overlooked. The staff of the Historical Section, Yale Medical Library; the Massachusetts Historical Society; and the Burndy Library, Norwalk, Connecticut, were extremely kind and helpful in locating resources for me.

Introduction

In his *Magnalia Christi Americana,* Cotton Mather chronicled the struggles of the early Puritan divines who immigrated to New England during Archbishop Laud's reign of persecution. Many of these early Puritans had obtained a basic knowledge of medicine and, once settled in the New World, provided medical care to their flocks. Mather characterized the combination of spiritual and secular duties in the preacher-physician as the *"angelical conjunction."*

Ever since "the days of Luke the Evangelist," observed Mather, "skill in *physick* has been more frequently professed and practised by persons whose more declared business was the study of divinity." He claimed that the healing arts were originally organized by church officials throughout the ages who "administered unto the *souls* of the people the more effectually, for being able to administer to their *bodies.*" While he referred to a long line of famous English bishops who had great skill in "physick," he argued that the "greatest frequency of the *angelical conjunction* has been seen in these parts of America, where they are mostly 'the poor to whom the gospel is preached,' by pastors whose compassion to them in their poverty invites them to supply the want of able physicians among them."

Although Mather's gift for hagiography is well known, historians generally have assumed that it was both the compassion of Puritan divines and the lack of trained physicians that made the "angelical conjunction" widespread in Puritan New England.[1] However, a number of factors previously unexplored converged in early New England to create an ideal environment for the proliferation of the minister-physician. This book explores those factors, emphasizing (1) correspondences and connections between religious and medical belief systems in colonial New England, and (2) similarities to and differences from the imported English model.

A number of early colonists noted the dearth of trained secular physicians in early New England, and records indicate that few professionally trained practitioners migrated during the seventeenth century. In the seventeenth century, the average ratio of medical practitioners to the general population of New England was about 1:1,000, with variations from region to region. Only during the eighteenth century did the ratio steadily increase to a high of 1:417 in 1780. By comparison, the ratio of healers to the English populace on the eve of the Great Migration was approximately 1:250 in the provinces and 1:400 in London.

When the Reverend Samuel Lee came to New England in 1686, he observed that the state of medicine was "very raw" there and that there were no "Licentiates" of the Royal College of Physicians, "no Lectures or instructors," and "no degrees in physick." He claimed that "[A]pot[h]ecaries doe practise what they will [,both] physick & Surgery" and said that surgeons belonged to no fraternity or guild, as in England, and had "no qualification but fro[m] their owne [surgical] chest & boxe."

While, by the end of the century, a number of practitioners trained through the apprenticeship method were serving the needs of the colonists, university-educated English physicians felt little impetus to transplant to New England when they were barely able to tend to the demands of their own well-to-do patients. Healers who, like Giles Firmin, had received some formal medical training in Europe found it difficult to earn a decent living in New England. Although many settlers were "very ill [of] . . . fluxes & fevers" in the town of Ipswich, Massachusetts, where Firmin lived, he wrote to Gov. John Winthrop in 1639 that he was "strongly sett upon to study divinitie; my studyes [in medicine] else must be lost; for physick is but a meene help." Competition was not a factor mentioned by physicians as an impediment to economic success in the embryonic years of the colonies of New England. Rather, most colonists, like the majority of residents in the English provinces they left behind, lacked the financial resources to seek a trained physician's aid.[2] Thus, English physicians could hardly be encouraged to migrate to New England, where they knew it would be difficult to earn the kind of salary to which they were accustomed. The lack of any significant number of European-trained physicians and surgeons in New England, even up to the time when Dr. William Douglass immigrated to Boston in the second decade of the eighteenth century, opened the medical market to the proliferation of not only the minister-physician, but also to a whole array of empirics.

One historian recently estimated that over 9 percent of all Puritan divines in New England were also physicians, while others have argued that all clerics practiced the art of healing during the colonial period. Because the records for many clergymen are incomplete for this period, it is difficult to know for certain what percentage of New England divines practiced medicine. This book's database consists of the records of 126 ministers known to have practiced medicine, mainly in the colonies of Massachusetts and Connecticut (see appendix 1). Because the emphasis here is on the relationship between Puritanism and healing in early New England, clerics have been selected from those colonies which represented the Puritan stronghold in the New World. Only in these colonies was the theology of the Puritans powerful enough to serve as the "theoretical foundation of the state as well as of salvation." Only in this region did Congregationalism dominate so completely through the end of the seventeenth century. The ministers shared a special kind of training (most were graduates of Harvard in the seventeenth century, of Harvard and Yale in the eighteenth), and, since most of them were Congregationalists, they believed in the same basic principles of religion, at least until the early eighteenth century.[3] All available secondary sources, as well as such documents as estate inventories, diaries, letters, church records, and sermons, have been consulted in an effort to analyze fully the angelical conjunction in New England.

One important factor which encouraged many colonists to seek the ministers' medical services was the widespread conviction that health and sickness were inextricably tied to sin and to the will of God. As Jehovah's chosen "ambassadors," the ministers served as his special arbitrators, helping both to heal the sick and to avert disease in their communities. When Thomas Symmes, minister of the congregation at Boxford, Massachusetts, visited the sick, many observed "that his *Prayers* with his People, were heard and come up for a Memorial before God; in restoring or preventing Sickness."[4] In the Puritan ethos, illness was a particularly meaningful affliction which struck with frightening regularity. Such episodes could be explained in a number of ways:

1. God was testing the faith of his children as he had tested Job.
2. An individual's personal sins had angered God, and the sickness He inflicted was an act of divine retribution.
3. In the case of epidemics, the collective sins of society often were blamed for God's vengeance.
4. Another person was thought to be responsible, often a "witch" in league with the Devil.
5. Satan's army of demons caused an illness.
6. Astrology or an unfortunate alignment of the heavens was to blame.
7. Natural causes were given—for example, when a man fell from the roof and cracked open his skull or when the weather accentuated an improper balance of the body's humors and so engendered disease.

Thus, there were supernatural causes, both divine and diabolical, and natural causes of disease. Often it was believed that a conjunction of two or more of these factors had produced sickness.

While, to the modern mind, such medical explanations seem like a bewildering quagmire, to Puritan divines the pathogenesis of illness was difficult but not impossible to understand. With personal and collective sin responsible for God's vengeance, it was the duty of divines to provide guidance to the afflicted and to urge them to realize that their own spiritual inadequacies might have led to their illness. God could be testing the faithful or punishing the wicked. How were lay men and women to know His intentions? While the laity was empowered with an understanding of the Bible and the principles of the Congregational Way, during times of terrible sickness and other hardships, the people turned to their minister for direction. This book explores some of the ways that the clergy interpreted and shaped the meaning of sickness for their flocks and examines the laity's shifting responsiveness, as New England developed into a modern, diversified society.

The intimate relationship between religion and healing in New England created an environment ideally suited to encourage the minister to combine prayer with practical medical techniques not unlike those used by lay practitioners. Yet compelling economic forces also motivated some clerics to serve as healers. Many of the earliest immigrant divines, aware of the highly unstable nature of politics and religion in seventeenth-century England, prudently had studied medicine before crossing the Atlantic. Being armed with two professions made it easier for them to make ends meet in this primitive and often harsh environment. After the middle decades of the seventeenth century, New England divines found it increasingly difficult to collect their full salaries from their communities, and many turned to medicine as a means of generating additional income. Toward the end of the seventeenth century and through the turbulent decades of the Great Awakening in the eighteenth century, New England churches and communities grew increasingly contentious. Many ministers were dismissed from their pulpits because their theological views failed to match those of their parishioners, forcing many to fall back upon their skill in medicine while they searched for another pastorate.[5] A minister's medical practice, therefore, could be the product of socioeconomic pressures, rather than a simple reflection of his "compassion to them in their poverty."

The second half of this book describes the minister-physician's understanding of the "secondary" or natural causes of disease; the kind of medical care these figures provided; the transit of medical, surgical, and anatomical knowledge from Europe to the New England clergy; and the differences and similarities between clerical healing practices and those of both regular practitioners and the more unorthodox "cunning folk." A study of patterns of medical-book ownership among minister-physicians and of their collections of personal remedies and other writings has revealed that two schools of medical thought dominated their medical thinking: Galenic humoralism and iatrochemistry (medicine based on chemical theories). While adherents to these two systems formed opposing medical factions in England, there is little evidence of such a debate in New England. Although they did not reject the basic tenets of Galenism (based on the balance of the four bodily humors), iatrochemical texts and remedies were very popular with Puritan divines. One important factor in this acceptance was the fact that the chemical arts, which during the seventeenth century were still fused with alchemy, were conceived of as being deeply religious in significance. Puritan divines collected iatrochemical texts that had a strong Calvinist tone which meshed well with their own theological views. Yet Galenism was not supplanted by the new chemical healing; rather, the mystical, religious aspects of iatrochemistry were separated from the practical side, and chemical medicines were retained alongside Galenic techniques and remedies.

The final chapter of this book explores clerical surgical practice and anatomical studies. Many ministers performed minor surgical procedures on their parishioners and also assisted in difficult cases of childbirth. Not uncommonly, they also witnessed or performed autopsies to determine the probable cause of death or to rule out the possibility of Satanic intervention.

Chapter 1

The Spiritual Physician

In the Garden of Eden, man was, in the words of the Reverend Samuel Willard of Boston, "suited to Immortality," until he sinned, and now "his health is lost, and from the very conception he is distempered and unhealthy, and so liable to all diseases" which are "ready to prey upon him."[1] For the God-fearing colonists of early New England, sickness and mortality represented the harsh sentence upon Adam and his posterity for failing to uphold the terms of Jehovah's first covenant with mankind. As expounded in the Bible and religious handbooks and by the clergy, the meaning of illness was linked to original and personal sin, as well as to the sinfulness of the body social. This chapter explores clerical efforts to define the relationship between sickness and sin in early New England. In this religious etiological framework, sickness could also be caused by witchcraft and demons. The clergy's role in diagnosing and treating diabolical distempers will also be explored in relation to lay expectations and lay participation in key episodes. Through pulpit, print, and private counseling, the clergy sought to heighten and mold the laity's understanding of sickness and healing as fundamentally religious phenomena. Clerical explanations of illness will be contrasted with those of the laity, in an attempt to determine whether or not distinct boundaries existed between the two groups' ideologies. Parallels with and divergences from the English precedent also will be highlighted, in an effort to characterize the uniqueness of the relationship between religion and healing in colonial New England.

When the Reverend Samuel Danforth spoke of the "great Physician of Israel" in an election sermon of 1670, the New England colonists understood the meaning of this "plain" metaphor. Their reading of the Bible had revealed that sickness and healing—both literal and symbolic—formed central motifs in both the Old and New Testaments. Particularly in Exodus and in the prophetic writings, the power of God to send and cure disease figures prominently. Jehovah had entered into a covenant with his chosen people, the Israelites, promising that if they would "diligently hearken to the voice of Yahweh your God, and do what is right in his eyes, and give heed to his commandments, I will put none of the diseases upon you which I put on the Egyptians, for I am Yahweh your healer" (Exodus 15:25b–26). His special treatment of the covenanted people came in the form of a bargain, and when broken, God retaliated with pestilences as judgment upon his wayward children. In Samuel 24:10–15, it is written that Yahweh struck down seventy thousand Israelites with the plague because David held a census against His will.[2]

The symmetry between God's treatment of the people of Israel in the Old Testament and his actions towards the colonists was strong in the minds of the New England Puritans. "Let Israel be the evidence of the Doctrine, and our glass to view our Faces in," the ministers insisted. The Puritans also saw clear parallels between contemporary England and ancient Egypt, and viewed themselves as God's chosen people in exile in the wilderness of the New World, the builders of the New Jerusalem. On board the *Arabella,* John Winthrop described New England's unique commission, in which the colonists had voluntarily and communally sworn to uphold all the laws of God in a national covenant. The Reverend John Cotton explained that, for upholding their part of the bargain, the people would be blessed with "health, maintenance, credit, prosperous successe in our callings and lawfull dealings, deliverances out of troubles, and such like." For seventeenth-century New Englanders, the concept of the covenant formed the basis of their organization of church and state. In addition to the national covenant, in which the colonists' obedience to biblical law was to be a product of free will, the individual churches which formed the backbone of New England society established their own covenants to uphold the laws of Scripture within each community, men and women formed a marriage covenant, and the Puritan had a personal covenant with God. The colonists understood that, once they had entered into the national compact, they were bound to uphold their commitment with a "strickt performance of the Articles contained" in the covenant. If they faltered, Winthrop warned, "The Lord will surely breake out in wrathe against us." The Bible had informed them that, when the Israelites violated the terms of their covenant, God retaliated with successive waves of affliction as punishment. As Thomas Hooker explained, "When God brings sore and wasting Calamities of Sickness, Famine, and War, on a professing people . . . God is not angry without a cause." As New England's guardians of the covenant, the clergy looked to biblical precedent and kept a watchful eye for signs of increased sinfulness in the land, which then informed their understanding and explanation of natural disasters, such as epidemics, as divine retribution.[3]

The Puritans' readiness to detect God's hand in the daily events of the natural world is an essential feature of their religion. They perceived an intimate relationship between the external world and the internal landscape of the soul. As the Reverend John Cotton explained, God "made this world to be a mappe and shadow of the spiritual estate of the soules of man: therefore . . . learne wee to discerne the signes of our owne times." While the writings of the clergy reveal a much more dramatic preoccupation with the divine meaning of natural occurrences, lay men and women also drew analogies between external events and inner experience. It was widely believed that an angry God drew upon an entire arsenal of natural manifestations of his wrath to dramatize his displeasure with his covenanted people, including hail storms, floods, drought, and "armys of Catterpillars" which destroyed the crops. In the clerical and lay ethos, disease was a particularly significant affliction sent by God. New England diaries, letters, sermons, and conversion narratives abound with descriptions of the successive waves of illness which often profoundly disrupted society. Yet understanding the meaning and etiology of disease, in their often complex relationships to collective and personal sinfulness and to covenant theology, was no simple matter. The clergy, as the authorized interpreters of the exclusive faith, felt it their sacred duty to familiarize themselves with the epidemics, as well as the individual ailments, of their parishioners so that they could interpret and justify God's will to the community.[4]

As early as the sixth century, the churchmen of medieval Europe had explained epidemics of plague as evidence of God's wrath at the collective sins of society. The theological interpretation of disease was designed to motivate the laity to be more concerned for spiritual than for physical well-being. In the words of Darrel Amundsen, theologians sought to "realign their [the laity's] well-being from a present horizontal to a future vertical orientation." The laity grew increasingly concerned with the eternal effects of God's wrath in the hereafter, and the plague was seen as a palpable indicator that the Last Judgment was at hand. With the plague as a powerful barometer of impending doom, an apocalyptic and millenarian mentality arose, one which the Puritans would inherit and dramatically amplify.[5]

To the modern mind, the medieval theological view of disease seems shrouded in ambiguity. A canon of the Fourth Lateran Council of 1215 cryptically stated:

> Since bodily infirmity is sometimes caused by sin, the Lord saying to the sick man whom he had healed: "Go and sin no more, lest some worse thing happen to thee" (John 5:14), we declare in the present decree and strictly command that when physicians of the body are called to the bedside of the sick, before all else they admonish them to call for the physician of souls, so that after spiritual health has been restored to them, the application of bodily medicine may be of greater benefit, for the cause being removed the effect will pass away.[6]

Although plague and, indeed, most epidemics were clearly linked to collective sin and an individual's general state of sinfulness could "sometimes" be the cause of sickness, in medieval theology specific sins rarely were pinpointed as causes of particular diseases. Richard Palmer has argued that, with the arrival of syphilis in Europe at the end of the fifteenth century, the "appearance of this new disease did much to provide factual support for the association of disease with sin."[7] Sexual immorality could cause one to contract the deadly syphilis; thus the connection of a specific sin to a specific disease may have bolstered the view that particular sins engendered sickness.

During the early modern period, the causal connection between sickness and sin crossed denominational lines, with both Catholics

and Protestants of various sects freely expounding the relationship between the two. The official organ of the Anglican church, *The Book
of Common Prayer* (1549), instructed the minister visiting the sick to
remind them that the form of their sickness was a result of God's will.
While some scholars have maintained that English men and women
of the early modern period rarely placed their illnesses within a religious etiological framework, others have suggested that Anglicans, as
well as many sectarians, subscribed to the compelling biblical evidence
that sin was connected to sickness and repentance to health. As the
prayer book was the most influential text of the Anglican church, it
seems likely that readers adhered to its assertion that sin played a causal
role in the pathogenesis of disease. To deny the equation of sickness
with sin was to deny the validity of the teachings of the Bible itself,
in which this connection was first drawn for Christians. A prayer to
be recited in time of plague or any other sickness petitioned: "Have
pity upon us miserable sinners, that are now visited with great sickness and mortality, that like as thou didst command thy angel [in the
time of David and the plague of the pestilence] to cease from punishing, so it may now please thee to withdraw from us this plague and
grievous sickness."[8] In order to stay the hand of Jehovah during times
of sickness, it was a precondition that those stricken admit that their
sinfulness was the just cause of their affliction.

William Perkins, an extraordinarily influential formulator of Puritan
doctrine in England (and no less revered in New England), maintained that, before the sick man called his physician, he should seek
out his minister, "for till helpe be had for the soule, and sinne which
is the roote of sickness be cured, physicke for the bodie is nothing."
Before he takes physicke, he must

> prepare his soule by humbling himself under the hand of God in his
> sickness for his sinnes, & make earnest praier to God for the pardon
> of them before any medicine come in his bodie. Now that this order
> ought to be used appeares plainly in this, that sickness springs from
> our sinnes as from a roote; which should first of all be stocked up, that
> the bra[n]ches might more easily die. And therefore Asa commended
> for many other things is blamed for this by the holy Ghost, that he
> sought not to the Lord, but to the physitians, and put his trust in

them. Oftentimes it comes to passe, that diseases curable in themselves, are made incurable by the sinnes and the impenitencie of the partie: and therefore the best way is for them that would have ease, when God begins to correct them by sickness, then also to begin to humble themselves for all their sinnes, and turn unto God.[9]

Although the Puritans condemned *The Book of Common Prayer* as a "dungheap full of popish abominations," they shared a similar theological interpretation of illness. Yet some have argued that there is a discernible difference between the Anglican and the Puritan ministers' methods of consoling the sick. In *The Anatomy of Melancholy* (1621), the cleric-physician Robert Burton contended that only Anglican ministers and physicians should attempt to cure those afflicted with melancholia. He believed that the Puritan's "spiritual physick"— which emphasized painful soul-searching to uncover particular sins deemed to be the provocation for illness, followed by a rigorous catharsis of sinful ways–could actually *cause* melancholia. Burton believed that, in conjunction with the ministrations of a good physician, "Faith, hope, repentance, are the sovereign cures and remedies, the sole comforts in this case; confess, humble thyself, repent, it is sufficient." Stanley Jackson recently argued that, "in contrast to the Puritan's condemnatory emphasis on sin . . . Burton's spiritual physick was a significantly more benevolent form of psychological healing." Yet while the minister-physician Richard Baxter (a victim of melancholia himself) believed that the cause of the disorder "is a conjunction of many sins," he also suggested that many were mistaken about the necessity for an almost masochistic sorrow over the sins that initially had caused the disorder. Many Puritans believed that "if their sorrow be not so passionate as to bring forth tears and greatly to afflict them," then they were not worthy of God's pardon. Baxter criticized those "unskilful teachers" who caused "the griefs and perplexities of very many."[10]

The Puritan clergy of New England did in fact encourage the sort of morbid preoccupation with sinfulness and its relation to illness which Baxter had decried. William Perkins–who formulated the federal (or covenant) doctrine upon which New England society was founded–suggested that ministers should spare no pains when urging parishioners to come to terms with their own sinfulness, because "by reproving in them some notorious sinne, that being pricked in the heart and terrified, they may become more teachable." Giles Firmin, a minister-physician who returned to the mother country for religious reasons, denounced the New England divines Thomas Hooker and Thomas Shepard for "polluting doctrine and causing seekers unnecessary anguish by casting distrust upon the first true motions of the Spirit." Firmin believed that New England ministers demanded more of the laity than God required, "calling upon them not to repent but to go beyond repentance, whereas the battle should be considered won as soon as men can lament their sins."[11]

New England divines used episodes of sickness—both individual cases and epidemics—as an opportunity to encourage good Christians to confront those personal sins which might have caused the affliction. During his ministry at Salem Village, the Reverend Joseph Green's son was badly injured in a fall. Green believed that "the sins which In th[i]s distress I cheifly was checked for, & repented of were *heart*-sins, & neglecting to pray so particularly and earnestly for my children as I should doe." Puritan theologians used illness and suffering as concrete indicators of the power of sin to corrupt not only the soul but the body itself. With health and healing entrenched in religious meaning, Cotton Mather believed that "a *Sickness* in the Spirit will *naturally* cause a *Sickness* in the Body."[12]

The diary of the Reverend Michael Wigglesworth, who was characterized by Edmund S. Morgan as a "morbid, humorless, selfish busybody," dramatizes the posture of the model New England Puritan, making it his Christian duty to look inward to uncover sin as a possible provocation for God to inflict illness:

> Gods visiting hand has now pluckt away 4 from us. . . . I had some serious thoughts about this token of the heat of gods great anger, my own sin kindling thereof. I came home and set my self seriously to meditate, and call over the sins of my whole life by a Catalogue . . . I am the man who sins to death gods precious servants . . . pardon my sin that I may not come into condemnation; neither visit my sins upon others. Rather let thy hand be upon me O Lord for my sins than upon these poor sheep whom thou afflictest, what have they done.[13]

Wigglesworth, a physically frail man who believed he was suffering from syphilis, in his diary reveals a commonly accepted tenet of his religion: New England Puritanism demanded that every member of the covenanted society actively participate in the extirpation of sin. And the first place that one should look when illness struck the individual or those close by was inward. "Ah Lord," Wigglesworth lamented, "I pul down evils upon others as wel as my self. Sickness, the death of godly ones, wants, divisions, have not my sins a hand in these miserys?" The Puritan's obsession with painstaking introspection in attempting to understand the outbreak of disease must be viewed in light of covenant theory. Because they had collectively promised to obey God's laws, and because the whole of New England was "legally" bound to His authority, the entire populace could be punished for the sins of any delinquent member.[14]

When a disease reached epidemic proportions within a community or colony, the clergy was quick to respond with allegations of rising sinfulness in the land. The church records of the Reverend John Eliot, the "Apostle to the Indians," are particularly rich in explaining epidemics as evidence of God's displeasure with his covenanted people. For the year 1647, he recorded that

> a great sicknesse epidemical, did the Lord lay upon us, so [tha]t the greatest p[ar]t of a town was sick at once, whole familys sick young & old, scarce any escaping English or Indian.
>
> The maner of the sicknesse was a very depe cold, w[i]th some tincture of a feaver, & full of malignity, & very dangerous if not well regarded, by keeping a low diet; the body solluble, warme, sweating, & c . . .
>
> Gods rods are teaching, o[u]r epidemical sicknesse of colds doth rightly by a divine hand tell the churches what o[u]r epidemical sp[iritua]l disease is. Lord help us to see it.[15]

Not only does this passage provide a typical example of the clergy's explanation of an epidemic as God's teaching "rod" upon the community for transgressions of the covenant, but also it shows the great detail in which the preacher-physicians described illness. In addition, we see the natural means probably used on patients to keep the "depe cold" under control. A variety of contagions plagued the colonists, including influenza, dysentery, and endless "pestilential" summer and winter fevers. However, countless cases of tuberculosis, pleurisy, colds, and other endemic disorders probably figured more significantly than epidemics in New England morbidity and mortality rates.[16]

In addition to trying to ameliorate by natural means the suffering of the afflicted (see chapters 4, 5, and 6), the clergy resorted to prayer in an attempt to soften the blows of the heavy hand of God during epidemics and other calamities. So that the entire community could atone for their "chiefe wrath p[ro]voking sins, as pride, covetousnesse, animositys, p[er]sonal neglecte of gospelizing o[u]r youth, & of gospelizing of the Indians & c., drinking houses multiplyed, not lessened, quakers openly tolerated," the ministers organized fast days which could be held throughout an entire colony or in particular towns, congregations, or households. Even individuals kept secret fasts to allow God to discover personal wickedness resulting from "original & actual sin." The practice of setting aside particular days for fasting to placate an angry God had become widespread in England after the Reformation. As in England, the Puritans in New England were strongly influenced by the precedent of Old Testament fastings.[17]

That a large portion of New England's fast and thanksgiving orders referred to epidemics indicates the profound impact that illness had upon colonial society. While the most dreaded afflication in the Old World had been the plague, for New Englanders it was smallpox, which came as a sudden and terrifying scourge and often forced the suspension of the regular activities of commerce and government. In England, smallpox had been endemic, a common yet dreaded affliction to which most of the population was exposed as children. In New England, the disease was sporadic, and the isolation of the individual towns often prevented it from being transported from one area to another. With each successive generation, the population grew steadily, rapidly producing new groups of non-immune children. The effect was a regular increase in the frequency of epidemics. When smallpox struck, therefore, it came in the form of deadly epidemics that terrorized the public.[18]

With the publication in the last decade or so of a number of studies of demographic trends in colonial New England, many historians have failed to appreciate the importance of epidemics in New England towns, claiming that throughout the colonial period such factors as epidemics were "so weak in their substance and so scattered in their incidence that they can best be considered as deviations from the norm, as 'accidents' within a larger framework of organic historical development." In the absence of Europe's double scourge of plague and famine, the communities of seventeenth-century Massachusetts and Connecticut have been characterized by some historians as "Peaceable Kingdoms" enjoying an abundance of land and freedom from internal, organized violence. As Timothy Breen and Stephen Foster have argued, "the existence of a widely accepted [Puritan] ideology strong enough to resist outside challenge, responsive political institutions, and general prosperity" largely explain the social cohesion of these colonies. These authors have suggested that the colonists experienced relatively good health and only a few epidemics in the first century of settlement, particularly along the port cities of the Atlantic coast.[19]

It is essential, however, to understand the Puritans' own assessment of the prevalence and meaning of sickness and disease in society. Clerical as well as lay writings reveal that sickness was ever-present, a phenomenon that received much attention in journals, letters, and sermons. Even the poetry of the day reveals particular distress over illness, especially when it struck innocent children. As Ann Bradstreet poignantly observed, the lives of children were fragile, "like as a bubble, or the brittle glass." Cotton Mather had fourteen children, losing seven shortly after birth, another at age two, and five in their twenties, and he was "in a continual Apprehension" that, although his son Samuel was a "lusty and hearty Infant," he would die in infancy. Samuel Sewall survived most of his fourteen children and was plagued by recurrent dreams of the death of his wife and children. In Edward Taylor's first marriage, he fathered eight children, and five of these died in infancy. He captured the profound impact of the terrors of sickness and death in the family when he described his own son's illness in verse: "But oh! the tortures, Vomit, screechings, groans,/ And six weeks Fever would pierce hearts like stone."[20]

While physical adjustment to a new disease environment can be traumatic in itself, in theocratic New England, the clergy underscored episodes of widespread sickness as evidence of God's mounting displeasure with his covenanted people. Urging confession and repentance, they hoped to restore spiritual health throughout their communities which would then improve physical health. While accidents and illnesses often were perceived simply as natural phenomena, the ministers attempted to see that the colonists' understood sickness and death in a religious framework. This was particularly important when the children of the settlers appeared to be slipping farther and farther away from their churches. In a thundering chorus, second-generation divines denounced the inability of their parishioners to bring their children into the churches, and warned that their backsliding would cause God to withdraw their "special appointment." Their church-state was to be as a "Citty upon a Hill," a model of Reformed Christianity, an example to the world, a beacon proclaiming the latter-day coming of the Messiah. Sacvan Bercovitch has argued convincingly that this litany of the New England divines differed significantly from the warnings of the English, which pertained only to mundane social matters, "to the city of man rather than the city of God." In New England, as never could have been the case in England or the other colonies of British North America, where religious uniformity did not exist, the purpose of this genre of sermons, known as *jeremiads*, was to "direct an imperiled people of God toward the fulfillment of their destiny, to guide them individually toward salvation, and collectively toward the American city of God."[21]

In 1662, the Reverend Michael Wigglesworth completed "Gods Controversy with New-England," in which he characterized an increase in sickness as evidence of God's displeasure with the backsliding of His covenanted people:

> One wave another followeth
> And one disease begins
> Before another ceases, becaus
> We turn not from our sins.
> We stopp our ears against reproof,
> And hearkin not to God:

> God stops his ear against our prayer,
> And takes not off his rod.[22]

During the second half of the seventeenth century, many New England ministers delivered jeremiads which often highlighted sickness as a palpable indication that the saints were straying from their covenant with God. As purveyors of this powerful ritualistic mode of castigation, the clergy helped create a climate of anxiety that was often manifested in a rather macabre preoccupation with the meaning of sickness and its relationship to sin.[23] The ministers believed that their environment had grown more "Epidemicall" and that the blame lay squarely on the shoulders of the people. The clergy actively sought knowledge concerning the spread of disease in their communities and guided their flocks to repentance through fasting and prayer, as a means of staying the hand of Jehovah, so that health and prosperity would again prevail in the covenanted society.

With their explication of disease as proof of God's anger over the failing mission of the second generation, the clergy urged not only prayer, fasting, and repentance, but also passivity. If, after much soul-searching, the saint could find no particular sinful cause to justify God's wrath, the Puritan was to bear humbly both his or her own illnesses and those of loved ones. John Eliot had been "exercised with [th]e Sciatica, & endured much anguish, dolour," but he looked upon his illness as an opportunity to grow closer to God "by the precious Visitation of his Spirit." The New Testament instructed the Christian that he would suffer under God's discipline and training, and that suffering actually was a prerequisite for salvation. According to the New Testament, the Christian was expected to view affliction as a cause for rejoicing for two reasons: "(1) God uses suffering as a means of producing spiritual maturity, if there is a right response to the affliction; and (2) the very fact that Christians endure suffering . . . is proof that they are the children of God." The act of suffering was rife with meaning for Puritans. The relationship between man and Jesus as loving and trusting—as emphasized in the New Testament—informed their understanding of physical affliction. Cotton Mather explained to his readers that "Suffering . . . belongs to the Compleat Character of a Christian." Thus, illness might be understood not only as a form of punishment for sin, but also as a particular demonstration of God's love and as an opportunity for his covenanted people to come closer to Him spiritually. The jeremiads actually may have catalogued Jehovah's "loving" punishments which served to confirm God's promise to his covenanted New Englanders.[24]

Regardless of whether the jeremiad traced the failure of the "errand," as Perry Miller has suggested, or whether the New England orthodoxy succeeded in transmitting the myth of the errand to posterity long after the theocracy had declined, the clergy lamented the decline of piety and observed a parallel increase in new and more virulent diseases. These the clergy felt were being visited upon the populace for breaking the covenant. In a letter of March 1761, the Reverend John Woodbridge, Jr., wrote that he was suffering from a "disease that then was Epidemicall (the change of our Manners in the wilderness from being heavenly to earthly and simply sincere and peaceable, to be cunningly sinfull and contentious, having changed our climate from Salubrious to unhealthy)." Cotton Mather also viewed New England's disease environment as a barometer of sinfulness, observing that it appeared "as if the Constitution of the *Earth*, and of the Air, and of *Humane Bodies*, has altered in Successive Ages; From whence *New Maladies* have arisen, which the praeceding Ages were Strangers to." Mather believed that smallpox was one of those "*New Scourges* . . . which the Holy and Righteous God has inflicted on a Sinful World." The reason, he explained, was because of a "Sinful Generation, a People Laden with Iniquity, a Seed of Evil-doers, Children that are Corrupters; They have forsaken the Lord! And why are ye Stricken more, Even with Strokes that were unknown to the more Early Ages? Tis because ye Revolt more and more!" Mather composed these words early in the eighteenth century, at a time when the populace indeed was revolting against clerical as well as secular forms of authority.[25]

How responsive were the colonists to clerical efforts to place illness and healing within a theological framework? There is evidence that lay men and women often linked their physical ailments, as well as illness and death in the family, to their own sinfulness. Ann Fitch of East Windsor, Connecticut, believed her father's death had occurred "because God was angry with me for my sins." The clergy fueled lay anxieties over illness, and sermons, as well as printed religious tracts, turned episodes of widespread illness into high drama. Many a conversion relation (a requirement of applicants to early Congregational New England churches, demonstrating the candidate's "visible sainthood" to the members) reveals that epidemics and episodes of individual sickness often precipitated a lay man or woman's conversion experience. In 1725, Abigail Strong related: "This spring when there was a mental distemper in this place, I was very much afraid that I should die as some of my neighbors did. I thought that God was angry with me and was afraid that he would take me away by death and that I should perish in my sins. I therefore sought God." Nearly half of the East Windsor conversion relations on record refer to sickness as the "means" of seeking salvation.

True to the concept of the covenant, lay men and women bargained with God during times of sickness, promising to serve the Lord more fervently if health were restored. In 1700, Hannah Bancroft Samuel related that "The first [spiritual] awakenings I had was when I [was] dangerously sick about four years ago, and then I made many promises, that if God would spare me I would be better and live another life." Some saw sickness as evidence of God's anger with their individual sins and as an opportunity to become better Christians; others were truly terrified that they would die in a sinful state and be tormented in the fires of Hell for all eternity. Ministers warned that "the Arrows of Death, the King of Terrors, fly so promiscuously among our mortal Race, that no Age, Rank or Condition of Men, is secure." Death could and often did strike suddenly; the preachers urged their listeners and readers to come to terms with God before death knocked at their door. Many lay people diligently read the Bible and religious books and listened to the preachings of the clergy, which reinforced their fears concerning sickness and death. While conversion relations are only representative of those individuals seeking full church membership, a step many colonists chose not to take, an examination of this genre supports the idea that clergy and laity shared a common understanding of the connection between illness and spirituality. Diaries such as those of Samuel Sewall also suggest that lay men and women often viewed their own sinfulness as the cause of sickness and death among their loved ones. Sewall buried eight of his children; when he learned that his wife had given birth to a stillborn son, he begged the Lord to "pardon all my Sin."[26]

While the thoughts of many pious colonists may have first turned to God during times of sickness, William Perkins, in *A Salve for a Sicke Man* (1596), criticized the English laity's initial reliance on natural medicine: "It is a thing much to be disliked, that in all places almost, the physitian is first sent for, and comes in the beginning of the sickness, and the Minister comes when a man is halfe dead . . . as though Ministers of the Gospell in these daies were able to worke miracles." Ronald Sawyer argues that diseases were "rarely placed in a divine etiological framework" in Elizabethan England. His penetrating new study of the medical practice of the Anglican minister and astrological physician Richard Napier (who worked in the southeastern Midlands of England in the early decades of the seventeenth century) reveals that most of Napier's patients, with the exception of those suffering from mental disorders, rarely talked about God in relation to their illnesses. Sawyer claims that, aside from plague, which was widely viewed as a scourge from an angry God,

> most somatic afflictions were either conceived in naturalistic terms, or attributed to some evil principle, ill spirit, or supernaturally nasty neighbor and did not correspond to any conventional theological doctrine. God was almost never seen as the perpetrator of disease by ordinary people and the lesson of Job had scarcely entered popular consciousness. . . . Nor were Puritan efforts to convert affliction into an occasion for examining the conscience of the afflicted successful. . . . Only in the case of mortal disease did religion seem to offer something that magic never could. Because of its comprehensiveness, religion could serve as an ultimate consolation and last resort when other remedies failed.[27]

Whether in England or America, the actions and thoughts of lay men and women during times of sickness are difficult for the historian to recreate. Although Rev. Napier's patients rarely may have discussed the theological implications of their ailments with him, the very fact that they sought the aid of a preacher-physician rather than a lay practitioner may imply a tacit understanding of disease as a religious phenomenon.

Were contemporary English men and women less likely than the New England colonists to adhere to clerical/biblical explanations and to view their illnesses within a religious framework? The New England milieu indeed differed from that of the mother country. Some historians have argued that two Christianities existed in much of medieval Europe and continued to exist into the early modern period, "the one that the clerics taught, the other of the peasants or the lower social orders." But a number of historians have argued convincingly that no clear demarcation between a "high" clerical and "low" folk culture existed in New England. It has been well documented that English emigrants who removed to New England in the seventeenth century were, for the most part, of "middling" status: they were not peasants but were artisans, merchants, yeomen, and their families—men and women "who knew how to articulate the principles of religion" because of an extraordinarily high rate of literacy. As one historian recently explained, "emigration simplified the cultural system by making it more uniform." As the colonists dispersed throughout New England and developed new settlements, Puritan divines accompanied them or were selected by the colonists to serve in their new communities. Thus the sociocultural milieu of the seventeenth-century New England colonies differed substantially from that of the mother country, because of the former's relatively uniform religious system and population. Richard Napier's clientele, which represented a cross-section of society, including peasants and noble men and women but lacking in Puritans, clearly highlights this disparity. To be sure, a systematic study of lay attitudes towards sickness and healing in colonial New England has yet to be completed. But, given the relative homogeneity of religion and society in seventeenth-century New England, as well as the confluence of lay and clerical attitudes concerning the relationship of sin and sickness, it seems likely that the colonists were more receptive to a theological theory of medicine than their counterparts in the more socially and culturally diverse mother country.[28]

In seventeenth-century New England, the clergy shared with the laity an understanding of health and sickness that was inextricably tied to the will of God. This understanding not only pinpointed sin as a cause of sickness, but also confirmed that witches and demons in league with Satan could be the progenitors of disease. Throughout the Christian world, in the early modern period it was commonly believed that Satan and his army of demons and witches could cause illness. This association was a product of biblical teachings. In Luke 13:11, Jesus described a woman possessed of a "spirit of infirmity" as one "whom Satan bound." Satan is cast as a perpetrator of illness in Acts 10:38; Jesus had the power to heal "all that were oppressed by the Devil" by expelling the demons. Although Christians believed that demons could cause disease, the Reverend Increase Mather explained "that Satan and all his wicked angels are limited by the providence of God, so as that they cannot hurt any man or creature, much less any servant of his, without a commission from him, whose kingdom is overall."

Richard Baxter believed that "most or many bodily diseases are by Satan; permitted by God," yet "there be causes of them also in the body itself." Thus Satan's ability to engender disease was bound not only by God's will, but also by the laws of nature. "When our own miscarriages, and humours, and the season, weather, and accidents may be causes, yet Satan may by these be a superior cause," Baxter explained. In cases of demonic possession, it was conceivable that a course of physick actually could cure a patient. In demonic melancholia, for example, Baxter argued that it was possible for medicines to cast the demon out, "for if you cure the melancholy, his [the Devil's] bed is taken away, and the advantage gone by which he worketh. Cure the choler, and the choleric operations of the devil cease. It is by means and humours in us that he worketh." The Puritans understood the etiology of disease as a complex interaction of primary and secondary causes: God was the first cause, and Satan operated under a "commission" from Him; while such factors as bodily disposition, the weather, and diet were viewed as secondary factors or causes in the medical framework.[29]

Belief in the powers of demons and witches was nearly universal throughout the seventeenth century. It was commonly accepted that "a near affinity between *Witchcraft & Possessions*" existed, because it was "by virtue of *evil Spirits* that *Witches* do what they do." New Englanders also believed that, through the aid of Satan, witches could cause people as well as animals to sicken and die. Cases of illness considered a result of *maleficia* were by no means unusual during the seventeenth century; in fact, European witchcraft accusations were often tied to episodes of sickness. The standard handbook on witches by two Dominican friars, the *Malleus Maleficarum* (1486), clearly revealed that witches could cause their victims "disease in any of the human organs" and "deprive them of reason" as well. When smallpox mysteriously broke out in Martha Carrier's family in Andover, Massachusetts, in 1690 and then spread to the rest of the town, she was held responsible and finally executed for witchcraft in 1692. During the trials at Salem, John Putnam accused Rebecca Nurse of witchcraft, claiming that his healthy eight-week-old son fell into "strange and violent fits" and died two days later as a result of her bewitchment. Another Salem victim complained of an act of *maleficium* which resulted in an infection in his foot, generating "several gallons of corruption" when lanced by a physician. Reflecting English precedent, cases such as these abound in the records of the New England witchcraft trials.[30]

How were the colonists to know when one among them was touched by an evil spirit? The *Malleus Maleficarum* advised that witchcraft could legitimately be suspected whenever the patient's symptoms failed to follow a classical disease pattern, natural remedies or procedures failed to induce a cure, or when an illness had an unusually sudden onset. In the New Testament, Jesus had separated ordinary illnesses from those caused by demonic possession: "People . . . came crowding in from the towns around about Jerusalem, bringing with them their sick and those tormented by unclean spirits, and all of them were cured" (Acts 5:16). While ministers, physicians, and magistrates agreed that it was imperative to distinguish between natural disorders and those that were supernaturally induced, establishing the distinction was no simple matter. Increase Mather explained that "sometimes indeed it is very hard to discern between natural diseases and satanical possessions; so as that persons really possessed have been thought to be only molested with some natural disease, without any special finger of the evil spirit therein." He described one baffling case where a man's illness "would have been judged no other than an ordinary epilepsy," but when he was stricken with seizures he could speak freely and rationally. Because the illness did not present the normal symptomology associated with epilepsy, a diabolical explanation was considered. In this particular case, "much means was used by skilful physitians for his relief, but without success for three moneths together." After this three-month regimen, the demon began to speak through the patient, and it "discovered many secrets both of the physitians and of other persons that attended." Not only did the patient's symptoms deviate from the traditional ones Mather associated with epilepsy, but also the patient did not respond to medication; the final diagnosis of demonic possession was then established when a demon reportedly spoke through the patient. Particularly in cases of epilepsy, prominent English physicians made similar supernatural diagnoses. Because epilepsy showed "no marks at all of the Morbifick Matter," Thomas Willis argued, "we may have deservedly suspected it [epilepsy] to be an inspiration of an evil spirit." The chief argument which fueled the association of epilepsy with witchcraft and the Devil was the biblical "proof" that Christ had cured an epileptic child possessed of an unclean spirit through exorcism, an argument which prevailed among many physicians even through the first half of the eighteenth century.[31]

Physicians often worked in tandem with ministers in making the distinctions between natural and supernatural ailments. After all, the *Malleus Maleficarum* stated that "if it is asked how it is possible to distinguish whether an illness is caused by witchcraft or by some natural physical defect, we answer that the first [way] is by means of the judgment of doctors." In contemporary England some conflicts occurred between these two professions over accusations of witchcraft-induced illness. In Essex, for example, a few physicians were skeptical about the powers of witches to cause illness, yet others doubled as cunning men and therefore were not likely to oppose such prosecutions. The so-called cunning folk were practitioners of "white" magic who specialized in finding lost goods and divining the future, but were especially known for their skills in healing. For the most part, it appears that English healers consulted when an illness was thought to be a result of *maleficium* collaborated with ecclesiastical authorities and eventually confirmed clerical diagnoses.[32]

In New England, the drama of a diabolical distemper unfolded within the community as a whole, with the minister, physician, patient, and his or her family playing the leading roles. The following two cases of possession and bewitchment illustrate the rich interaction between these individuals and the rest of the community in which they lived, and demonstrate the penetration of supernatural beliefs into all levels of society. In 1671, the Reverend Samuel Willard began to record the account of the bizarre possession of Elizabeth Knapp, his sixteen year-old maidservant. Before her violent convulsions began, he had "observed oftentimes a strange change in her countenance, but could not suspect the true reason, but conceived she might be ill." Her affliction began when Willard was away, and she begged for the minister of nearby Lancaster, Connecticut, to come pray with her. Upon Willard's return, she confessed her many sins and claimed she was tormented by Satan himself, who relentlessly badgered her to sign her own name to "a book, written with blood, of covenants made by others with him." About a week after the onset of her convulsions and odd behavior, Willard called in a physician in consultation, "who judged a maine part of her distemper to be naturall, arising from the foulnesse of her stomacke, & corruptnesse of her blood, occasioning fumes in her braine, & strange fansyes." He prescribed a course of physick, and she experienced a remission of nearly three weeks, but then her condition worsened, and the fits grew more violent. Willard related that the "Physitian being then agen with her consented that the distemper was Diabolicall, [and] refused to administer [medication], [and] advised . . . extraordinary fasting; whereupon some of God's ministers were sent for." Once the physician's course of physick failed to cure her and he finally agreed with Willard's diagnosis of demonic possession, the case was left in the hands of her pastor, who prayed for her recovery. While the final outcome of this episode remains unknown, Elizabeth insisted that she be taken to Boston so that a large assembly of ministers could pray with her in the hopes of driving Satan from her body.[33]

This case illustrates how supernatural explanations of physical disorders had penetrated all levels of early New England society, from servants to magistrates and clerics. The possessed girl even participated in her own diagnosis and treatment: it was she who called in a nearby minister when Willard was away and confessed that she was tormented by Satan. She also demanded to be taken to Boston to receive the healing "power" of concentrated clerical prayers. In addition, the community knew the details of her case, and many volunteered to attend her in her afflictions. Her neighbors flocked to watch the bizarre spectacle, and some even attempted to speak to the demon that "possessed" her. Others sought to help diagnose the particular cause of her ailment, toying with the idea that it was the result of witchcraft.

When the physician attempted unsuccessfully to cure Elizabeth by natural means, his failure only strengthened the assumptions of the possessed girl, her minister, and the townspeople that she was in fact touched by an evil spirit. Even her doctor recommended recourse to such religious forms of healing as fasting and prayer. As John Demos argues, Willard was her "clergyman therapist," and his treatment consisted of prayers and efforts to make Elizabeth confess her sins. While Satan was understood as the ultimate cause of her affliction, there is evidence to indicate that Willard and the townspeople of Groton eventually concluded that the girl herself was a sinner, and only through confession could she hope to be rid of the yokes of evil.[34]

The involvement of the community in episodes of supernatural affliction was also an important aspect of the Salem witchcraft proceedings. The Reverend Samuel Parris had consulted a doctor when his daughter and niece suffered from unusual "fits"; the physician believed that they were "under an Evil Hand," and a minister related that "this [diagnosis] the Neighbours quickly took up, and concluded that they were bewitched." After bewitchment was confirmed, lay men and women often relied upon ancient folk tests to uncover the witch, including the baking of urine cakes and the scalding of the sick child's urine.[35]

With the publication of his *Memorable Providences, Relating to Witch-crafts and Possessions* (1689), Cotton Mather unwittingly may have fueled the Salem witchcraft crisis. He described in lurid detail an episode in Boston in which the four children of John Goodwin were "sadly molested with Evil Spirits." Once again, the suspicion of witchcraft in this case was indicated by the impairment of the children's health through *"Strange Fits*, beyond those that attend an *Epilepsy*, or a *Catalepsy*, or those that they call *The Diseases of Astonishment."* Naturally, in their distress, the parents of these children contacted Mather, the minister of their church. He in turn consulted with local "Skilful Physicians," including his "worthy and prudent Friend Dr. *Thomas Oakes"* who was "so affronted by the Distempers of the children, that he concluded nothing but an hellish *Witchcraft* could be the Original of these Maladies." Once his supernatural diagnosis was confirmed by a "prudent" and respected physician, Mather could legitimately proceed with the cure. While the children's parents claimed they had been approached by many who offered unorthodox means of assistance, the Goodwins "rejected all such counsils, with a gracious Resolution, to oppose *Devils* with no other weapons but *Prayers* and *Tears*, unto HIM that has the chaining of them." Cotton Mather gathered together a group of four of the Bay Colony's most powerful and respected ministers, and together with some "devout Neighbours," he led them in a day of fasting and prayer in the home of the afflicted children. "The children were miserably tortured, while we laboured in our *Prayers*," wrote Mather, "but our good God was nigh unto us, in what we call'd upon Him for. From this day the power of the Enemy was broken. . . . The *Liberty* of the children encreased daily more and more, and their *Vexation* abated by degrees; til within a little while they arrived to *Perfect Ease.*" As John Goodwin related, in such cases as this, *"Doctors* cannot help," because the affliction of his children was *"more than ordinary*, it did certainly call for *more than ordinary* Prayer." Only the consolidated and extraordinary powers of such Puritan luminaries as the Reverends Cotton Mather, James Allen, Joshua Moody, Charles Morton, and the veteran demon-fighter Samuel Willard—together with some of the more pious lay members of the community—could drive the demons from the children's bodies. The

involvement of this community in demon-fighting once again illustrates the lack of distinct boundaries between clerical and lay religious
ideologies. In addition, true to the Puritan ideal, John Goodwin
blamed his own sinfulness as the cause of his children's afflictions.
Because he hadn't admonished and instructed his children enough in
matters of religion, he believed that "God was hereby calling my sins
to mind, to stay my Children. . . . I thought I had broke Covenant
with God."[36]

   With the children's hellish maladies cured, Cotton Mather hyper-
bolized the superior healing abilities of Puritan divines through the
publication of his best-selling *Remarkable Providences*. While the clergy
publicized these episodes in an effort to bolster their crumbling authority in the colonies, they also sought to validate their own orthodox techniques of healing the supernaturally afflicted. The Protestant
Reformation had stripped the clergy of its "magical" and most powerful weapon against Satan's demons: the rite of exorcism. In every in-
stance where illness is linked to cases of demonic possession in the
New Testament, Jesus is said to have cured the infirmity through exorcism. Because of popular demand, exorcisms abounded in England
even after the Reformation, particularly in sectarian circles. Although
forbidden to perform this "popish" ritual, the Protestant clergy could
use prayer as a powerful healing tool. Placing an unprecedented emphasis on the terrifying presence of the Devil in the world, Protestant
clerics urged prayer, fasting, and repentance in the face of witchcraft
or possession. As the cases of Willard and Mather above have demonstrated, Puritan clergymen engaged in "practical divinity," or the cure
of souls, to treat demoniacs and the bewitched. If a parishioner's
disease were indeed sent by "Daemons, as Instrumental Causes," then
the natural methods of the physicians often proved useless. Through
the spoken and written word, the clergy confirmed and heightened
popular belief in the oppressive and tangible presence of Satan in the
world around them, characterizing themselves as God's chosen gener-
als leading the community in never-ending battle against the seduc-
tive Prince of Darkness.[37]

   Although Protestant clerics were forbidden to perform exorcisms,
the ritual continued to be conceived by the masses as a powerful

counterattack on evil spirits. On both sides of the Atlantic, many forms of countermagic were widely used against illnesses and other afflictions thought to result from bewitchment and demons. Mather admitted that the Goodwins had been approached by individuals who made them "Many *Superstitious* proposals" to help cure their children. And during the witchcraft proceedings at Salem, one Mary Sibley, a church member, was publicly censured for baking a "diabolical" cake of rye meal and the urine of the possessed children in an effort to determine who had bewitched them. The colonists often nailed horseshoes above their doors to keep witches out of their homes. The use of countermagic by both "cunning folk" and church members was by no means unusual in seventeenth-century New England.[38]

Often the target of clerical aggression, the cunning folk were commonplace in Tudor and Stuart England and had even "infiltrated" Puritan New England. Throughout the seventeenth century, English and colonial divines condemned the practice of white magic as deriving from the same satanic origins as maleficent witchcraft: "One artificer hath devised them all," claimed the Reverend Richard Bernard. In fact, many divines argued that white witches were even more dangerous than their malevolent counterparts, because, while many people shunned the evil witches, they flocked to the cunning folk for healing; in doing so, they placed their very souls in peril. In England, however, the clergy's condemnation of the satanic nature of these healing practices fell, for the most part, on deaf ears. Individuals from all social classes, many of them convinced that the powers of these practitioners were divine gifts, continued to resort to the cunning folk in order to be healed of their many illnesses. While church authorities were unanimous in proscribing these healers' activities, legal action rarely was taken against these individuals. Many historians have rejected the assumption that popular culture in England and much of early modern Europe was isolated and malleable and passively followed the dictates of the clergy and state. Instead, historians have posited a reciprocal and mediating influence between "popular" and "elite" culture. Clive Holmes argued recently that the "acceptance of the cultural products of the [English] elite depended less upon the vigor of the missionary efforts of divines and lawyers, than upon the fit between their concerns and the needs, aspirations, and intellectual expectations of the populace." The continuing popularity of the cunning folk must be ascribed to their functional utility, as well as to cultural values and expectations.[39]

How widespread were the cunning folk in New England? Cotton Mather charged that "the *Sacraments of Hell* are particularly observed, in the *Sorceries*, wherewith many ungodly and unhappy People seek the Cure of their *Diseases*. . . . and upon Use of odd and mad *Charms*. By the *Charms*, of *Words* and *Marks*, and the like, which tis plain can be of no *Natural Efficacy* for the Cure of Diseases, People in short plainly go to the *Devil* for a Cure." In his sensationalistic style, Mather claimed that "millions of unadvised People, have surrendered themselves unto Satan" through a variety of publications which provided the reader with healing charms and instructions for creating magical amulets. Mather wrote these words in the 1720s, and even at this late stage in colonial development, he charged that such practices were commonplace, even "among those who have been *Baptized* for God." Mather explained that the reason for the popularity of the cunning folk was that "people often find a strange Releef of their *Maladies*" through their efforts. "The Spirits of the *Invisible World* . . . are, no doubt, very *Skilful Physicians*" and "help them to some Ease of their Distempers," he continued. If the clergy believed so strongly in the healing powers of "sorceries" and "charms," the stock and trade of the cunning folk, then obviously the laity shared their views. "How frequently is *Bleeding* Stancht, by writing something, with Some Ceremonies, on the Forehead! How frequently is a *Toothache* Eas'd, and an *Ulcer* Stop'd, and an *Ague* Check'd, by Papers, with some *Terms* and *Scrawls* in them, sealed up and worn about the Neck," Mather wrote. Yet, no matter how effective such remedies were, the clergy argued, such practices demonstrated an *"Implicit Covenant* with the *Devil."* Mather quoted Ecclesiastes and argued that *"The Lord has created Medicines* out of the Earth, and he that is wise will not abhor them."[40] Mather believed it was imperative for divines to provide spiritual counseling in their communities during times of illness and to circumvent the use of "diabolical" charms and the other supernatural techniques of the cunning folk, by promoting the use of natural cures.

But, like the efforts of the laity he served, a minister's healing efforts could overstep the boundaries of orthodoxy. In the Anglican Richard Napier's extraordinarily popular and pluralistic medical practice, he often recited traditional prayers with his patients, yet he also incorporated folk formulae containing pre-Christian as well as Catholic elements. Napier was deeply immersed in the occult and developed quite a reputation as a practitioner of Cabala magic. He claimed he conversed with the archangel Raphael for advice when making prognostications for the sick, and he sought the unorthodox aid of angels when purging the demons from those patients whose illnesses he considered preternatural in origin.[41]

In the Bay Colony, Philip Nelson, minister of the church at Rowley, Massachusetts, and a graduate of Harvard in the class of 1654, created an uproar by attempting to cure a deaf boy "in imitation of our Savior, by saying Epphatha." Jesus originally had used the Aramaic expression *Ephphatha*, meaning "be opened," to heal a deaf mute (Mark 7:34). In Massachusetts, the ministers of neighboring congregations were called together, and the boy was brought before them so that they could determine if he could speak. The child was interrogated, but "there he stood, like a deaf and dumb boy as he was!" The Puritans believed that the days of miraculous healings as reported in the New Testament (which served to validate and authorize the mission of Jesus) had ceased long ago. While the Apostles "by their *miraculous operations*" set "the *Seal* of Heaven to the Doctrine they taught," their Protestant successors were heirs to the Apostles' ministry "in their *ordinary* Capacity only." The Protestant was encouraged to seek natural means to cure ailments, to confess his or her sins, and to pray to God for relief. Yet they were forbidden to use religious and/or pagan incantations to effect a cure. To ecclesiastical authorities, the incantation of prayers so often performed by the cunning folk during their healing rituals implied a superstitious belief in the magical powers of words, without God's assistance, and constituted a practice repeatedly condemned in the Bible.[42]

A widespread belief in the supernatural powers of the clergy had survived the Protestant Reformation and had stolen into the New World through the Great Migration. The Reverend Hugh Adams assumed the ministry in Durham, New Hampshire, early in the eighteenth century, and shortly thereafter he was accused of praying to God for a drought as retribution against the town for their failure to pay his salary. The community grew enraged over his unorthodox utilization of his religious "powers"; eventually he undid his "spell," causing the heavens to burst forth with much-needed rain. While Keith Thomas has argued that the "Reformation took a great deal of the magic out of religion," he has traced the activities of numerous English "sorcerer-parsons" in the Tudor and Stuart periods and even into the nineteenth century. Such well-known minister-physicians as Richard Burton and George Herbert advised that when the English parson visited the sick, he should preface his cures with prayers, "for this is to cure like a Parson, and raiseth the action from the Shop, to the Church." Thomas has suggested, however, that the use of prayers in healing "could easily degenerate into superstitious reliance upon their unaccompanied efficacy."[43]

It would appear that some of the religious healing methods utilized by divines in both the old country and in New England could be as unorthodox as those of the cunning folk officially condemned by ecclesiastical authorities. In fact, it is often difficult to differentiate the practices of the cunning folk from those of the legitimate practitioners of medicine and divinity in New England. One December evening in 1747, the Reverend Ebenezer Parkman's son fell asleep by the fireplace and accidentally slipped from his chair, badly burning his hands in the fire. "For his relief," Parkman wrote, "I immediately kill'd a Cat and he wash'd his Hands in the Blood."[44] If this incident recorded by Parkman in his diary had happened fifty to sixty years earlier, his actions could have aroused suspicion that he was practicing witchcraft. While his remedy may not be characterized as "black" magic, it certainly speaks to the survival of magical vestiges in American folk medicine, even among the clergy.

Many of the medical remedies used by clerics and laity alike seem to border on the occult. As will be discussed more fully in chapters 3, 4 and 5, a remarkable network for the exchange of medical remedies existed in colonial New England, as in the mother country. For example, many ministers collected unusual cures from local women with reputations as healers. From "Sister Blower," the Reverend Thomas Symmes obtained several "Receipts for Worms in Children," a common problem in colonial New England; she advised him to take "Garlic 3 cloves, Rotten Eggs, Rye meal" which should be "laid to the soles of the feet."[45] While much more evidence needs to be gathered, many such remedies no doubt came from the cunning folk, perhaps indicating a reciprocal influence or leveling between clerical and popular ideologies of healing.

The colonists of seventeenth-century New England shared with their ministers a theological framework for understanding and diagnosing illnesses. Physical sickness was linked to the spiritual health of the individual as well as to that of the body social. As the second generation slipped farther and farther beyond the grasp of the clergy, ministers grew increasingly vocal in characterizing New England's disease environment as a gauge of sin and God's resultant retribution. Increases in sinfulness and disease indicated that Satan had a powerful and growing hold on the people. New England divines stood firmly upon biblical authority in ascribing some illnesses to satanic intervention, and the laity, believing the word of God, shared these assumptions. Through the spoken and written word, Puritan divines stimulated and confirmed the popular belief that demons and witches caused physical illness. And for opportunists such as Cotton Mather, the "clergyman-therapist's" role in diagnosing and curing diabolical distempers dramatized the clergy's superior healing powers and authority in all matters touching upon religion.

While the laity may have accepted the clerical-biblical association of illness with sin, demons, and witches, lay people were extremely eclectic in the means they chose to seek health. Those who publicly professed that an episode of sickness had led to a conversion experience, or that their sins had engendered their own ailments or those of their loved ones, in private actually may have clung to unorthodox medical practices. While Elizabeth Knapp believed that her sins might have been a factor in her demonic possession, the townspeople (including some full church members) relied on ancient folk tests to uncover the witch behind her affliction. The colonists also resorted to countermagic and the remedies of the cunning folk in an effort to combat diabolical distempers, and possibly to treat everyday ailments as well. Cotton Mather and the more orthodox of the Puritan divines publicly condemned the healing remedies of the cunning folk as satanic; yet, as in England, the continued popularity of such remedies among the masses attests to the independence of the laity in selecting medical treatments. So, although lay men and women may have shared with the clergy basic assumptions about the etiology of illness, and although they participated in communal fastings and prayers to help stay the hand of Jehovah during epidemics or when one among them was possessed or bewitched, ancient folk traditions had made their way across the Atlantic with the Great Migration and remained entrenched among the people. Lay men and women may have perceived no contradiction in their medical eclecticism, perhaps because they rejected clerical condemnations of the healing practices of the cunning folk as satanic in origin. While nailing a horseshoe above the door was viewed as a means of keeping witches (and the illnesses they could cause) away, it is doubtful that those who performed this ritual believed that their actions placed their souls in peril. Recent studies of the popularity of the cunning folk in England also indicate, at the popular level, a rejection of the antipathy of divines to white magic and a selective acceptance of "elite" concepts. This pattern of medical selectivity may have extended to the clergy as well, for there is evidence to indicate that some ministers also overstepped the bounds of medical orthodoxy, further narrowing the gap between the clergy and the people of New England in matters of sickness and healing.

Chapter 2

"For Service or for Selfish Gain?"

While the ministers of colonial New England have been portrayed as isolated figures in their communities, holed up in their studies crafting learned sermons by the fireside, their diaries and letters reveal that they often spent considerable time and energy visiting and consoling the sick. The minister's frequenting of homes in his community brought him into intimate contact with the sorrows and sicknesses of his flock. Since the early Middle Ages, the visitation, care, and comfort of the sick had been among the clergy's responsibilities. Serious illness was the obvious precursor to death, and the cleric was expected to attend the dying, to administer last rites, and to help them come to terms with the final judgment at hand. Often the most educated members of rural communities, many clerics possessed a rudimentary knowledge of the medical arts and felt a responsibility not only to provide spiritual guidance to the afflicted, but also to administer remedies to help heal their tortured bodies.[1] Yet the clergy's motivation for pursuing the art of healing in addition to their religious duties was multifaceted. Such factors as the association of religion with healing (discussed in chapter 1), a lack of trained practitioners in many rural areas, the inability of the poor to afford secular medical care, and a clergyman's desire to boost his income from medical practice all contributed to the proliferation of the cleric-physician in England from the Middle Ages through the early modern period, as well as in the British colonies of New England. An examination of the various factors influencing the English precedent of clerical medical practice serves to illuminate the transference and unfolding of this phenomenon in early New England.

During the early Middle Ages, Christianity emerged as a religion of healing, and it brought about a major shift in society's attitudes toward the sick. Although early Christian literature stressed that it was the duty of all believers to attend the sick and poor, a growing number of men and women in religious orders provided medical treatment in their communities. In response to the New Testament imperative to extend care to the sick as an act of Christian charity, various monastic orders founded hospitals. In their treatment of illness, the early priests of medieval England drew upon the precedent of the numerous healing acts performed by Jesus and his disciples in the New Testament. Jesus was known as the "Physician both of Soul and Body," and Christians believed that both soul and body became "ill" and required healing. As Henry Sigerist explains, Christianity "addressed itself to the disinherited, to the sick and afflicted, and promised them healing, a restoration both spiritual and physical." In his *Summa Theologica*, Thomas Aquinas said that "the theologian considers the nature of man in relation to the soul, but not in relation to the body, except in so far as the body has relation to the soul." Christian men and women believed that God had allowed physical suffering in the world as a result of original sin; that he punished particular sinners as well as sinful nations with disease; and that he tested the faith of his believers through trials of sickness as he had done with Job. With the health of the body intertwined with the state of man's soul, the theologian could intervene legitimately at both the corporeal and spiritual levels in cases of sickness. One historian recently suggested that, in early modern Europe, "acceptance of disease as a function of the wrath of God, of healing medicine as a function of His mercy, and of the physician as His instrument, would indicate the *priest*-physician as the norm."[2]

Boasting of the lengthy association between the professions of medicine and divinity, John Ward, a preacher at Stratford-on-Avon and a well-known physician, made the following entry in his diary in 1660: "300 years agoe," medicine was "not a distinct profession by itself, but practisd by men in orders, witness Nicholas de Ternham, the chief English physitian and Bishop of Durham; Hugh of Evesham, a physician and cardinal; Grysant, physician and pope; John

Chambers, Dr. of physick, was the first Bishop of Peterborough; Paul Bush, a bachelor of divinitie in Oxford, was a man well read in physick as well as divinitie, hee was the first Bishop of Bristoll." Indeed, during the fourteenth century, Englishmen who obtained any formal education in medicine often had taken at least minor religious orders. Huling Ussery has argued that most of the eminent physicians of Chaucer's time were secular clerics, while a minority were monks, friars, Jews, clerks in minor orders, and laymen.[3]

Robert S. Gottfried's recent survey of over two thousand English medical practitioners who lived in the period from 1340 to 1530 reveals that 12 percent of those practicing in the fourteenth century were clerics, while by the following century only 6 percent of the group had taken holy orders. Breaking down his practitioners into physicians/leeches, surgeons, barber-surgeons, barber-tonsors, and apothecaries, he suggests that this downward trend in the numbers of clerical practitioners may be explained by the rising numbers of surgeons, barber-surgeons, and barber-tonsors, almost all of whom were uneducated laymen. "By 1500 medicine was a secular career," Gottfried argues. While admitting that 25 percent of the physicians in his group had taken holy orders, that 46 percent of those physicians who had attended university had taken some sort of holy orders, and that 12 percent of all physicians attending the royal family were also clerics, he maintains that the clergy did not represent the driving force in medicine that many historians have suggested. However, based on his own study and those of other historians, it would appear that clerical practitioners in fact were highly visible within the ranks of healers. Margaret Pelling and Charles Webster have even suggested that, given the striking numbers of transfers between the two professions, and the fact that so many men pursued careers in medicine and divinity simultaneously, "priest-physicians constituted a dominant group in the medical profession" as late as the sixteenth century.[4]

As the universities developed during the late Middle Ages, secular physicians increased in number and importance in society, and medicine emerged as an organized profession. Although the medical profession became increasingly secularized over the course of the Renaissance, many clerics continued to practice medicine. Even after the Protes-

tant Reformation and the closing of the monasteries in which the ancient medical learning of the Greeks had been preserved, many English
ministers still combined their clerical duties with the art of healing.
Particularly in rural areas, English men and women continued to resort to the minister to be cured of many of their illnesses, often for
such pragmatic reasons as the high cost of secular medical treatment,
but also, no doubt, because of the timeless connection between physical
and spiritual healing.

During the seventeenth century, prominent Anglican and Puritan
divines alike voiced the opinion that the minister should provide
medical care to his parishioners. In the Anglican preacher-physician
George Herbert's celebrated advice to the English clergy, *A Priest to
the Temple or, the Countrey Parson* (1633) (a work popular among Anglican and Puritan divines on both sides of the Atlantic), Herbert suggested that it was the parson's professional duty to provide health care
to those sick parishioners who could not afford the fees of regular
physicians. He argued that it was "easie for any Scholer to attaine to
such a measure of Phisick . . . by seeing one Anatomy, reading one
Book of Phisick, having one Herball by him." He suggested that by
gaining a knowledge of nature's countless medicinal herbs, the parson
could witness the "manifold wisdom of God" wonderfully displayed.
To study medicine, as well as the natural sciences in general, was to
know God through his magnificent earthly creations. The New England
divine John Cotton also characterized the study of natural philosophy
and medicine as a religious act in itself. He explained, "To study the
nature and course, and use of all Gods works, is a duty imposed by
God." It would reveal not only the greatness of God, but also would
benefit mankind, "both of body for health, as in the knowledge of
many medicinall things; and of soul for instruction."[5]

Medicine also was given a high priority in the Puritan utopian treatises of mid-seventeenth-century England. In the *Macaria* (1641), Ga-
biel Plattes argued that the clergy should take an active role in secular
affairs, unlike Catholics in holy orders, who isolated themselves from
the community in monastic seclusion. He envisioned that, in the
perfect society,

the parson of every parish is a good physician, and doth execute both functions, to wit, *cura animarum & cura corporum*, and they think it as absurd for a divine to be without skill of physick, as it is to put new wine into old bottles; and the Physicians being true Naturalists, may as well become good Divines, as the Divines doe become good Physicians.

In millennial expectations of the Great Instauration of man to a state of complete equilibrium with God and nature that existed before the Fall, the Puritans' knowledge of medicine played a very important part. In the restoration of man's dominion over nature, they believed that, through the aid of God, man would discover the secrets of health and sickness and gain control over the body's ailments. A healthy body was conceived of as both a precondition for and a reflection of spiritual health. Once the mysteries of physick were uncovered, man conceivably could increase his lifespan to a thousand years. Therefore, as Charles Webster and others have argued, millennial ideas inherent in Puritanism stimulated Puritan interest in the medical sciences.[6]

In New England, Puritan divines were expected to attend the sick in their communities. Cotton Mather prepared a guide for Puritan divines outlining their responsibilities towards those parishioners with infectious diseases. Entitled "Concerning the Obligations lying upon Ministers of the Gospel to 'Visit the Sick,' in times of Epidemical and Contagious Diseases," the guide suggested that "when a minister is well assured that the sick of his own flock are laboring under such loads upon their conscience as cannot fitly be unburdened unto any but himself, he has a call from Heaven to venture himself to the utmost for the service of such a soul, and may expect the protection of Heaven accordingly to be a shield unto him." However, in the Reverend John Allin's (HC 1643) account of the great plague of London in 1665, he revealed that "above 7 score drs, apothecarys, and surgeons are dead of this distemp[er]," and a surprisingly large number of ministers also became victims of the plague from visiting their patients. The New England clergy understood that they were obligated to attend to the spiritual needs of their flock even if they were victims of an epidemic, but they sought to limit their exposure to those who were infected because of a legitimate fear of contagion. Their pastoral guide suggested that the minister should consult his congregation to determine "whether they are willing that he should sacrifice his life unto the private services of the sick," and that one minister should be chosen to visit the sick of all the towns within a specific geographical area.[7]

On the other hand, during the smallpox epidemic of 1721, Benjamin Colman was convinced that, while the clergy was fulfilling its professional responsibilities by visiting and consoling the sick, the ministers often were responsible for spreading disease, "call'd from day to day, to the many noxious Chambers, each of which have had poison eno' in 'em to have spread the Town over." Colman drew upon current advances in microscopy and mechanical theory (iatromechanism) in his understanding of contagion. He was convinced of the existence of a "Multitude of Animalcules," which he called "Animated Atoms," and which he believed caused the "common Infection" of smallpox. Thomas Smith (HC 1720), minister of Falmouth, greatly alarmed his community "for visiting Mrs. Cox, who was broke out with the smallpox," even though he had done so at the request of the justices and selectmen. His contact with an infectious case made the community afraid that he could serve as an agent of infection in his pastoral visits to other homes in the region, which caused "Several families" to move away "for fear of the small pox." When the Reverend Ebenezer Parkman (HC 1721) received two letters from friends who had just been innoculated for smallpox, he immediately burnt them both for fear of catching the disease from them. He also had obtained a recipe to prevent infection from letters received in the mail, which called for immersing them in vinegar and then drying them in smoke. Although the mechanism of contagion was not clearly understood, clergy and laity alike had a general sense that diseases such as smallpox could be communicated from one individual to the next through "secondary" or natural means. Yet it was generally understood that God was the "1st and best cause of all things" and that he expressed his will through the agency of the natural world.[8]

Puritan divines had a responsibility not only to visit the afflicted during epidemics (unless their parishioners urged them not to) but also to inform the public about patterns of infectious diseases raging throughout the colony. Even if a minister did not practice medicine, he had an obligation to alert the people of his community, often during his Sunday sermon, to the deadly progression of contagious diseases in other regions, and to make predictions as to whether or not his own area would be affected. Some clerics, typically medical practitioners as well, also advised the public on the best means of treating such diseases as smallpox when they were raging in epidemic form. In response to an outbreak of 1676–77, Thomas Thacher, the pastor of the Old South Church in Boston, prepared the first medical broadside published in British North America, entitled *A Brief Rule to Guide the Common People of New England how to Order Themselves and theirs in the Small Pocks or Measels* (Boston, 1677). Thacher was familiar with the writings of the "English Hippocrates," Thomas Sydenham, and he drew almost exclusively upon his medical writings for the people of New England. He recommended "moderate keeping" of the patient, which entailed allowing nature to do her own work, a moderate diet, without an overabundance of blankets and hot cordials ("hot keeping"). Thacher also referred to the "circulation of the blood" and advised against a hindrance of this process, indicating his familiarity with William Harvey's discovery, first published in 1628.[9] Thus, in addition to a responsibility to visit the sick, even during epidemics, the clergy also felt an obligation to inform the public through pulpit and print of the best measures to treat these deadly infections.

With societal and professional expectations that the minister should visit and care for the sick in his community – whether in Old or New England – came the opportunity for a preacher-physician to permeate lay culture with his religious views. The influential English divine and physician, Richard Baxter, claimed that he took on the care of the sick in his parish during an outbreak of pleurisy and took not "one Penny" for his efforts. He found that his free administration of physick was a "very great advantage" to his ministry, because it made his parishioners feel obligated to hear him preach his weekly sermon. And when a Quaker family of Boston became ill, Cotton Mather jumped at the opportunity to pay them a "medical" visit, to "releeve them and instruct them, and do all the Good that is possible for them," in the hopes of softening their hearts toward the Congregational Way.[10]

Thomas Mayhew, Jr., of Martha's Vineyard, one of the ministers

who pioneered the missionary movement to christianize the Algon-
quian tribes of early New England, practiced his medical skills on
potential converts. In one case where an Indian was "very sick of a
Feaver," Mayhew "bound his arme, and with Pen-knife let him blood;
he bled freely, but was exceedingly faint, which made the Heathen
very sad; but in a short time, he began to be very cheerful, whereat
they much rejoyced. . . . and it pleased the Lord the man was in a
short time after very well." Mayhew confessed that his provision of
health care to the Wampanoags "hath advantaged my progresse" and
was a vital factor in luring the Indians away from their shamans and
encouraging their acceptance of Christianity.[11]

Medicine was a powerful tool for the minister in converting the
uninitiated and keeping good Christians within the fold. When many
New Englanders fell ill, they were highly motivated to seek out and
accept the services of the preacher-physician, because health and sickness were viewed within the context of religion. The first minister of
Milton in the Massachusetts Bay Colony, Peter Thacher (HC 1671),
recorded in his diary in 1682 that "Father Tucker told me he did verily
believe he was the better for my prayer, the day before, for the fever
presently left him, & [the] swelling of his legs was down."[12] The clergy's
medical ministrations often were performed in a holy fashion which
served to elevate these efforts above those of secular physicians. And,
perhaps more important, the ministers' patients reportedly felt the
power of prayer was an aid to recovery.

Without denigrating the benevolent aspects of clerical medical practice, another important factor motivated many clerics to practice the
healing arts: the need or desire to supplement their incomes. While
Cotton Mather claimed that the angelical conjunction was a commonplace phenomenon in New England because the ministers' "Compassion to them in their *Poverty*, invites them to supply the Want of
Able *Physicians* among them," many combined the professions of
divinity and medicine because of financial pressures. After graduating
from Harvard College in 1697 and entering the ministry, Hugh Adams
was plagued with a series of tumultuous and unhappy pastorates,
chiefly because, he complained, his parishioners' "Sacrilegious Cov-

etousness & fraud" cheated him of his full salary. To compensate for his financial difficulties, Adams looked to biblical precedent: "As I perceive, Luke the Beloved Physician (as he is named in Col.IV.14) was maintained by his Practice of Physick while he preached the Gospel freely; so I trust in the same Providence for my personal and family sustenance."[13] After the middle of the seventeenth century, New England clerics found it increasingly difficult to collect their full pay in their communities, forcing many to turn to medicine to make ends meet. An examination of the socioeconomic factors behind clerical medical practice in early modern England and the emergence of a similar set of circumstances in the changing milieu of colonial New England reveals the less "angelical" and more mundane character of this widespread phenomenon.

During the Middle Ages, it was not uncommon for clerics to engage in a secular occupation, particularly medicine and law. Although the New Testament encouraged the provision of care to the poor as an act of Christian charity, some clergymen engaged in these professions as a means of generating income. During the twelfth century, in an atmosphere in which commercial and professional activities escalated in intensity and variety, the Church expressed concern over the propriety of the cleric's acceptance of payment for medical or legal services rendered. Avarice replaced pride as the supreme vice, leading Church authorities to ask one important question regarding secular pursuits by the clergy: "Was it undertaken for service or for selfish gain?" Ecclesiastical authorities observed that an "evil and detestable custom" had emerged:

> monks and canons regular, after having received the habit and made profession, despite the rule of the holy masters Benedict and Augustine, study jurisprudence and medicine for the sake of temporal gain. . . . they are led by the impulses of avarice. . . . the care of souls being neglected and the purposes of their order being set aside, they promise health in return for detestable money, and thus make themselves physicians of human bodies.

Canon law forbade monks and canons regular to pursue the study of law and medicine for the purpose of financial gain, yet these canonical prohibitions had little lasting effect and applied only to those clerics who were professed religious and therefore were expected to withdraw from the affairs of the world. By the following century, a clerical medical treatise (written to instruct the clergy so that they could provide care to the poor *gratis*) argued that it was quite acceptable for the clergy to receive fees from their wealthy patients. It was no secret that physicians were the wealthiest of all the so-called middle-class occupational groups of the period, including lawyers.[14] Although many priests and monks (particularly those in the mendicant orders) undoubtedly took no pay for their medical services, others obviously looked upon the medical profession as an opportunity for "selfish gain."

Throughout the early modern period, many clerics continued to engage in the art of healing. Practicing two professions could generate a substantial fortune for ministers with a wealthy clientele. The Tudor physician Thomas Linacre owed his prosperity to the juxtaposition of these two occupations, as did Lancelot Browne, William Harvey's father-in-law. While some clerics amassed riches from the fat purses of their well-to-do patients, they appear to have been the exception rather than the rule. The majority of clerical salaries in sixteenth-century England were woefully inadequate; to make matters worse, this income was usually in the form of tithes that often proved very difficult for the minister to collect. In the county of Derbyshire, three-quarters of clerical incomes assessed in 1535 were valued at less than ten pounds per year. A century later the situation had changed, with well over one-third of clerical livings capable of supporting a minister. However, most seventeenth-century divines were college graduates with a wife and children to support. In contrast to the earlier period, now there were unprecedented demands on income and new expectations of a comfortable professional lifestyle. Surprisingly, clerics in urban areas often suffered most, because of their dependence upon the town corporation for a meager financial endorsement and upon sporadic and often paltry payment for individual sermons. Rosemary O'Day has discovered that while

a large number of rectors were keeping their heads above water economically and even prospering as a result of rising prices, a great number of the country's 3,800 vicars were remaining impoverished and in real terms being more stretched than ever, as families and changing life-styles made their relentless demands. . . . One can only speculate as to how far the . . . curates were in the seventeenth century even more than previously compelled by poverty to engage in by-occupations.[15]

Rural clerics often turned to agricultural pursuits, and their often impoverished status reflected that of the community they served. In larger and wealthier parishes, some clerics began to enjoy a more flam-boyant lifestyle, one which mirrored that of the lesser gentry. Radical anticlericalism both before and, especially, after the Civil War was bolstered by the observation that ministers formed a distinct caste because of their university training and professional interests. Of course, many ministers enjoyed an amiable relationship with their parishion-ers, but some of the latter resented the clergy as "watchdogs" of the establishment and strict disciplinarians. Clerical tithe litigation rose during this period, evidence that it became increasingly difficult for the minister to collect his pay in the community. In a vicious cycle, the litigation further fanned the spreading fires of anticlericalism.[16]

Even by the end of the seventeenth century, nearly half of the benefices of the Church of England were valued at less than fifty pounds. As a means of compensating for these insufficiencies, many clerics practiced as healers in order to supplement their meager church incomes. The cleric Robert Burton, who authored the *Anatomy of Melancholy* (1621) and confessed to dabbling in the medical arts as well, explained that "many poor country vicars, for want of other means, are driven to . . . turn mountebanks, quacksalvers, empir-ics." A modest church income was not always a reflection of a parson's theological views: Independents, Presbyterians, and Anglicans alike often combined the two professions. One of the most famous Anglican cleric-healers of the Tudor period was Richard Napier, a man whose medical services, during the early part of the seventeenth century, were greatly sought after, in part because he charged very low fees for his health care. He charged about twelve pence for a medical visit, which roughly corresponded to a laborer's daily earnings.[17]

The seventeenth century witnessed periods of profound societal upheaval which, fueled by warring Protestant factions, finally erupted into civil war during the middle decades. As the religious affiliations of those in political power shifted, divines of different theological views were persecuted. Clerics of various doctrinal affiliations prudently studied the art of healing, in case their primary means of support was temporarily or permanently lost. A number had acquired medical skills during their student years through private study, from classmates learning medicine at the university, by witnessing anatomies, or through informal apprenticeship to a local healer or herbalist. Throughout the seventeenth century, English clerics lived with an often profound sense of insecurity, fearing that their particular theological views soon might go out of favor. Aware of the unsettled condition of church and state, a minister often would learn medicine as a second occupation, not only to bolster a paltry clerical salary, but also to rely upon for a living during times of persecution. English clergymen were often realistic professionals who recognized that their positions were at best tenuous. Protecting themselves and their families with two occupations, they could struggle through politically unfavorable periods until they could return to their chosen profession of divinity.[18]

Dissenting divines in particular suffered extraordinary persecution by the authorities, both before and after the interregnum (when Puritan factions reigned). After the Act of Uniformity of 1662, over 1,700 Nonconformist ministers were driven from their pulpits for rejecting the Anglican *Book of Common Prayer* and for refusing re-ordination by a bishop of the Church of England. This was not the first time such a purge had taken place, nor would it be the last. Similar ejections had occurred under Queen Mary, Queen Elizabeth, King James I, during the interregnum, and another took place after the Revolution of 1689. Thus the clerical profession had been plagued with uncertainty and instability from the turbulent years of the Protestant Reformation through the latter part of the seventeenth century.[19]

Edmund Calamy's *Account* (1702) of those Nonconformist divines ejected under the Act of Uniformity of 1662 reflects a particular sensitivity to their sufferings. Only a hundred or so (out of 1,760 ejected) possessed the security of private means, and the loss of their pulpits forced most to seek another way to feed their families. As Richard Baxter observed after losing his pulpit, "It pierceth a Man's Heart to have Children crying, and Sickness come upon them for want of wholsom food." The majority defied the law and preached in their homes or in those of their supporters, and faithful listeners paid them what they could for their individual sermons. Some were lucky enough to have wealthy benefactors or to receive payment from Presbyterian relief funds, while the less fortunate were fined or imprisoned for their illegal preaching. Not a few grew so depressed that they could not even preach the gospel. One minister "was fain to spin as Women do, to get something towards his Family's relief (which could be but little); but being Melancholy and Diseased, it was but part of the Day that he was able to do that." Of those ejected, it has been estimated that 101 (6 percent) taught school, while 59 (4 percent) turned to the practice of medicine. Only a few turned to trade and farming. An enterprising divine might even combine professions: John Brent, who had been chaplain of Magdelan College, "had several young Gentlemen under his care, and preach'd occasionally, as well as practis'd physick." He died quite wealthy, with an estate valued at 1,537 pounds. And John Reynolds, formerly minister at Wolverhampton, Staffordshire, was "eminent for skill in Divinity, Physick and Law"; his estate was valued at over 2,000 pounds because of the "noble and rich Patients, that made use of him as a Physician," according to a contemporary.[20]

The fortunes of those who turned to the medical arts varied considerably. Some decided to take a medical degree to help establish a more secure practice, but, because the English universities were officially closed to Nonconformists, most studied abroad. Yet the possession of a medical degree was no guarantee of success. Francis Cross took his degree at Leiden and then settled at Bristol to practice medicine. He died penniless and in debt over two hundred pounds.

Others managed to use their medical practice to their political advantage, by winning over the local authorities. Giles Firmin had returned to England from the Massachusetts Bay Colony and ministered to a congregation in Colchester, Essex. After the purge of 1662, he "practis'd Physick for many years and yet was still a Constant and Laborious Preacher. . . . And he held on thus, in the hottest part of King *Charles's* Reign, having large Meetings when so many other meetings were suppress'd." The reason that Firmin managed to continue to preach without persecution was that he had "one considerable Advantage above his Brethren, which was the Favour and Respect which the Neighbouring Gentry and Justices of Peace had for him, on the Account of their using him as Physician." He was widely respected by such influential members of the community in part because he "took but very moderate fees" for his medical services. By charging his patients the Puritan's proverbial "fair price," he failed to secure an estate for his heirs, which, according to Calamy, "had been a very easie thing" to obtain from a medical practice as successful as his.[21]

Immigration to New England became an attractive alternative for those dissenting clerics who had been forced by rampant religious persecution to pursue a second occupation in England. A number of Puritan clergymen who eventually transplanted to New England had learned the art of medicine "on a foresight of the ruin of the clergy" in their homeland, to provide them with a second occupation in case they were forced out of ministerial office. John Fiske had entered the ministry after his graduation from Cambridge in 1628, and soon afterward Archbishop Laud's silencers were upon him for nonconformity. He then wrote to John Winthrop that, "seeing the danger of the Times," he had "changed his profession of divinitie into physic, [and] was licensed" for medical practice. Fiske quit the ministry until he immigrated to the Massachusetts Bay Colony, where he successfully combined the two occupations in the new settlement of Wenham.

Ezekial Rogers had helped engineer the settlement of Roxbury in 1639, and he too described the atmosphere in England before his immigration as a time of the "hottest persecution" by that "bloody hierarchy." Being "enlightened concerning the evil and snare of subscription and ceremonies," Rogers had been advised "to give over the thought of the ministry" and to switch to "the study and practice of physic." He was relieved when "the Lord mercifully prevented that," because, in his opinion (like many other Congregationalists), although medicine was "a good and necessary calling," he had observed that "the most, through their own corruption, have made it to themselves the very temptation to covetousness or lust, or both." In *The Countrey Parson*, George Herbert referred to the "general ignominy . . .

cast upon the profession" of medicine. Because of the reputations of many English physicians as greedy opportunists who preyed upon the miseries of the people, some Puritan divines felt more comfortable with the healing arts as an adjunct to their clerical careers. Although Rogers had been advised to take up medicine because of his dissenting views, in addition to practicing physic, he continued to preach secretly in the home of an "honourable family" until he could safely and openly perform both duties after his immigration to the New World.[22]

Men like Fiske and Rogers came to New England to escape Archbishop Laud's silencers in England and for the right to minister to a congregation in a fashion that reflected deeply-held religious beliefs. They also hoped to find financial security within their calling. Yet many found it necessary to continue practicing physic because of a new set of economic constraints in the New World which led to an early replication of the British model of paying the parson for his medical care. Once in New England, the unusual and time-consuming manner in which Puritans established their churches often made it necessary for the clerical candidate to fall back upon another occupation while awaiting ordination. Although the majority of first-generation ministers received ordination within a year of their "call" from a community, when John Fiske left the town of Salem to help establish the new community of Wenham in 1640, he reverted to lay status until he received his official ordination from the new congregation four years later. In the meantime he had to earn a livelihood, so he relied upon his medical skills as well as farming to support himself and his family. Therefore, it was to a minister's advantage financially to have skill in both divinity and medicine when making the decision to remove to the New World, because it often took a year or more for a town officially to settle a minister. Other delays in the formation of new churches in early New England were attributed to the fact that, since the Antinomian crisis, the magistrates and elders of neighboring churches had had to sanction the proposed congregation, in order to avoid the proliferation of unorthodoxy in the Holy Commonwealth. Of course, by definition, the Congregational Way called for a slow and cautious movement in forming a new church. With the adoption of the Cambridge Platform in 1638, the process was standardized somewhat, yet communities were extremely conscientious and exacting in choosing a minister, typically listening to the sermons of many would-be pastors before ultimately selecting the one most suited to their collective taste.[23]

In the late 1650s, Puritan divines grew increasingly alarmed by the observation that the preaching of the word was generating few new conversions. A Synod of 1662 led to the widespread introduction of the "half-way covenant" which extended baptism to the children of those who had been born and baptized in the church but had not discerned the effects of saving grace in their lives. These individuals then could retain partial church membership without being allowed to participate in the sacrament of the Lord's Supper. The half-way covenant generated a heated controversy over the decline of "purity" in New England's churches and brought into the foreground the difficulties inherent in the Congregational Way of gathering churches. As a result, throughout New England, dissatisfied factions withdrew from their churches and established separate congregations with ministers whose views coincided more closely with their own.[24]

After the Synod of 1662, ministers assumed even greater control in their communities as the powers of the congregation became attenuated. Perhaps pastors felt justified in encroaching upon these powers because of the influx of "graceless" men and women into their congregations through the half-way covenant. Nevertheless, as the clergy refrained from seeking the church's consent in making important decisions, they embarked upon an "open departure from the fundamental Congregational principle that authority rested ultimately with the saints." As a result, towns often took even longer to make their choice of a minister, for fear of selecting a candidate who would overstep his authority. The laity deliberately imposed these lengthy delays in ordaining second-generation ministers, in an attempt to gain more control over the actions of the clergy. The town of Durham, Connecticut, postponed the ordination of the minister-physician Nathaniel Chauncey (HC 1661) for five years, finally requiring in writing that he consult the congregation when making decisions important for the community. Naturally, as with so many other ministers during this period, his skill in medicine supported him until his ordination.[25]

If a candidate found a suitable position in a particular region, he would often "wait it out" and refuse other offers. In fact, men of the cloth often were as particular in selecting a pulpit as the townspeople were in selecting their parson. During the interim, if the candidate had possessed the foresight to study the healing arts, he could support himself through medicine and, having already established a clientele, could then supplement his income through medicine after assuming his pastorate.

One important factor in a town's choice of a particular minister may have been his possession or lack of skills in medicine. The Reverend James Clegg (1679–1755), a Nonconformist divine of Chapel en le Frith, England, had taken up farming as well as the practice of medicine to supplement his meager clerical income (which was less than thirty pounds per year). The nearby town of Bolton was debating whether or not to offer him the ministry of the church, but the people were divided over the issue of his medical practice. "Many of them are unwilling to have one who practices Physick," he recorded in his diary in 1729, and "it was not then thought proper" to give him a call. Clegg's medical practice had grown steadily over the years. He treated the poor and "middling" as well as the richest of families; his patients were of varying religious persuasions and came from a wide geographical area seeking his services. On one occasion, "an ancient man came for [medical] advice . . . on foot, about 36 miles." A practice as large as Clegg's constantly interrupted his primary responsibility: the salvation of souls. "My Practice of Physick I find has taken up much of my time and cost me a good deal of pains," admitted Clegg during an episode of deep soul-searching. "I hope to do some service that way to God and my neighbours, but that is not the work I was chiefly devoted to. My ordination vows are still upon me and I ought to take more pains for the salvation of souls and to lay out my selfe more for promoting the edification and salvation of those that are committed to my care."[26]

During the early years of New England's settlement, most towns were too poor to pay the salary of a minister as well as a physician. Perhaps the candidate with medical training used his additional skills as a bargaining chip to secure a higher salary. On the other hand, the ability to draw a separate income from medicine actually may have resulted in a town's contracting the minister for a more modest salary. The Reverend John Rogers (HC 1649) assisted in the ministry in Ipswich, Massachusetts, but his salary was lower than his associate's because he was engaged in a thriving medical practice. He continued preaching there, explained Cotton Mather, "until his Disposition for *Medicinal Studies* caused him to abate of his Labours in the *Pulpit*," perhaps because medical practice was more lucrative.[27]

Soon after their arrival in New England, many first-generation ministers complained that it was difficult to make a decent living from the voluntary contributions of the community they served. The Massachusetts Bay Company had established a fund to provide for the maintenance of the ministers, but in 1630 it placed the burden of a minister's maintenance on the individual towns. No legislation provided guidelines for the determination of a minister's salary or for collecting it, so each town was forced to work out the details on its own. The colonists had brought to America a bias against the problematical system of tithing that predominated in England. As a result, the towns initially chose a system of voluntary maintenance, which, in the eyes of such leading divines as Richard Mather and John Cotton, most resembled that of the pristine years of the early Christian church. Unlike Mather and Cotton, but much like their colleagues across the Atlantic, other preachers soon began to complain bitterly about inadequate support by their communities. Charles Chauncy grumbled to the governor and assistants of the Massachusetts Bay Colony over his impoverished condition as preacher to the town of Scituate. He claimed that he lived in "actual want even of some of the necessaries of life," not having enough bread to feed his family of ten. In 1654 he assumed the presidency of Harvard College with a salary of one hundred pounds a year but again found it difficult to provide for his family and put five sons through college. As a preacher of the word, Chauncy previously had relied upon his medical skills for additional income, yet he claimed that his duties at the college required "the whole man, and one free from other distractions" such as the need to engage in the healing arts. He repeatedly petitioned the General Court to raise his salary, but was again forced to "take his liberty upon other [financial] opportunities."[28]

While the clergy grew increasingly vocal in its dissatisfaction with the system of voluntary maintenance, those members of a community who lacked full membership in their local churches also complained about having to pay the salary of a minister. Feeling the financial pinch of supporting him, even full members began to grumble over having to dig deeply into their own pockets when they could barely eke a living from the rocky New England soil. After consulting with the clergy, the Massachusetts General Court responded to this crisis by enacting legislature in 1638 which stipulated that "every inhabitant in any town" could be "compelled" to pay his share of the minister's salary if he failed to do so voluntarily. The Connecticut and New Haven Colonies soon enacted similar legislation, followed by Plymouth in the 1670s. As the towns abandoned the voluntary system, they were forced to rely upon taxation to insure the collection of the minister's salary. With the formulation of the Cambridge Platform, the clergy demanded that the magistrates make certain that the "ministry be duly provided for." Early in the settlement of New England, then, the Puritan ideal of voluntary maintenance of the ministry proved unrealistic. The magistrates responded to the colonists' opposition with legislation which institutionalized the minister's ability to collect a covenanted salary, leading John Cotton to remark that "when magistrates are forced to provide for the maintenance of ministers, etc., then the churches are in a declining condition."[29] So began the ministry's lament over the declension of piety in New England.

Second- and third-generation ministers increasingly turned toward the use of written contracts between themselves and the towns that hired them, in order to obtain a good salary and a secure position. In spite of some difficulties in collecting their salaries, immigrant ministers of the first generation who practiced medicine had a higher percentage (81 percent) of pastorates free of public controversy than any subsequent generation until the Revolutionary era (see table 2.1). By the second generation, only half of these ministers managed to avoid heated arguments with their parishioners over such issues as salary—arguments which often led factions within the membership to demand the pastor's resignation. The clerics therefore sought binding contracts to institutionalize their authority and gain some stability. The town, however, also utilized these "covenants" to gain control

Table 2.1
Controversial or Peaceful Ministries Among Preacher-Physicians

(N=126) Group No.	Not Available (Percent)	"Peaceful" Ministry (Percent)	"Controversial" Ministry (Percent)
1 (1630–1650) N=14	0.00	81.25	18.75
2 (1651–1670) N=12	18.75	50.00	31.25
3 (1671–1690) N=11	9.09	72.73	18.18
4 (1691–1710) N=15	6.67	60.00	33.33
5 (1711–1730) N=23	4.55	45.45	50.00
6 (1731–1750) N=29	0.00	58.62	41.38
7 (1751–1770) N=22	4.76	80.95	14.29

Note: The seven groups are broken down by the time periods in which the ministers in this study first began their professional careers. The term "'Peaceful' Ministry" refers to a pastorate with no record of public arguments between the minister and his flock. A "'Controversial' Ministry," on the other hand, denotes a pastorate where arguments between the minister and his people were recorded.

over the minister, by, for example, setting a limit on the number of years he would serve, with the decision to renew the agreement resting in the hands of the pastorate.[30]

New ministers arriving from the mother country received the most sought-after pulpits in New England, and a strong majority of Harvard-educated second-generation candidates for the ministry were forced to seek work in less desirable areas, such as in the towns along Long Island Sound or in communities with a notorious history of quarreling. In the classes graduating under Harvard's first two presidents (the classes of 1642–71), 111 graduates entered the ministry, and 74 (66 percent) of these served in at least two different pulpits. A number of factors contributed to make this group less stable geographically than the immigrant clergy of preceding generations. Contentiousness in the congregations frequently led to dismissal. Unlike immigrant ministers, who often accompanied their flocks from England, these natives lacked a bond to any particular parish. There was a shortage of pulpits in the 1640s, and preference was given to immigrant ministers. All these forces converged to make second-generation ministers as a group more mobile than their ancestors. (See appendix 2 for mobility patterns of minister-physicians.) As David Hall and others argue, of all these factors, unprecedented contentiousness in the towns was the single most important reason for the high turnover of ministers. Although, during the seventeenth century, New England was relatively united in its commitment to uphold the national covenant which dictated the limits of acceptable behavior, the towns never eradicated the petty bickering observable in most societies past and present.[31]

Many of Harvard's early graduates who intended to enter the ministry came of age in a period of economic instability in New England. Because immigration to New England virtually ceased by 1645, the formation of new towns had temporarily ground to a halt, suppressing the demand for new ministers. Still fresh in the minds of these young men's fathers was Archbishop Laud's reign of persecution before the overthrow of the monarchy. This precedent, in conjunction with New England's own economic crisis, proved a powerful stimulus for those choosing the precarious path of the ministry. Many second-generation Harvard graduates preparing for a career in divinity took up the healing arts, like many of the first generation before them, not merely to provide medical services to their parishioners out of Christian charity, but as an alternative or adjunctive means of generating income. During the depression in New England which paralleled the interregnum, many second-generation Harvard graduates who intended to enter the ministry were forced to travel to England in search of a pulpit during a politically favorable time when church and state were controlled by the Puritans. Those graduates who journeyed to England were well aware that, while the political milieu was congenial to dissenting divines under the Long Parliament, their theological views soon could be out of favor. While many of these Puritans obtained positions in the ministry in England during the politically favorable years of the Protectorate, most were ejected after the Restoration, when the Act of Uniformity (1662) was enforced.[32]

Isaac Chauncy traveled to England during this period and managed to obtain a position as minister of a Congregational church at Andover. Not surprisingly, he was ejected and later prosecuted as a "seditious person" for his illicit preaching. His father had prudently trained his sons for the dual path of divinity and medicine because of his own financial difficulties as a Massachusetts minister. Isaac wisely obtained his license from the College of Physicians so that he could legally practice medicine in the city of London. Thus, like their fathers before them, second-generation graduates of Harvard often chose the dual path of the minister-physician to help them through difficult times.[33]

In the face of rampant anticlericalism (which closely resembled the English precedent) and difficulties in collecting their full salaries, many preacher-physicians found it increasingly difficult to continue in their double capacity. Cotton Mather claimed that Michael Wigglesworth relinquished his ministerial duties at his Malden parish because his "Sickly Constitution so prevailed upon him as to confine him, from his Public Work," for many years. Yet Wigglesworth privately drafted a manuscript entitled "Some Grounds & Reasons for laying down my office Related," which revealed a number of other forces at work that caused him to step down from the pulpit and continue with his medical practice. He admitted that one of the major reasons for this move was that his ministry was a contentious one: "I find that of late the

more I have laboured for their good the worse I am requited. Especially by most unjust & hard censurs past upo[n] all my administratio[n]s.
So that I see no place for doing [them] any further good. . . . of late
yeers their incouragements have been real discouragements, as hold-
ing forth contempt or at least a very low esteem of my ministry." He
did admit that he was in a weakened physical state, but the reason
for this development was that he had been financially forced to pursue "Two different callings so different in their nature [i.e. medicine
and divinity], & both so weighty [and] . . . too heavy for one mans
shoulders, especially one so weak." Wigglesworth admitted that the
angelical conjunction simply was too much for him to handle. He
chose to continue with his medical practice rather than divinity, he
argued, because it was through the former that he "mainly & almost
wholly depend[ed] upon under god for an outw[ar]d subsistance."[34]
Wigglesworth's private explanation for temporarily relinquishing his
ministerial duties is indeed enlightening and suggests that the con-
vergence of a number of factors led to his decision: his health had
been adversely affected by combining two income-producing professions; his ministry was a contentious and unhappy one; and most of
his income was generated through his medical practice anyway. So he
chose to continue it rather than the clerical path.

   After the adoption of the Saybrook Platform in Connecticut in
1708, the clergy established a system of county ministerial associations in order to settle the communities' many disputes with their
parsons. The Saybrook Platform attempted to strengthen clerical authority by placing more power in the hands of the ministers, thereby
clearly undermining the power of the congregation. Lay resistance to
the authority of these Presbyterian-style associations was profound, and
contentiousness in the churches increased. The clergy continued to
be attacked by their flocks, with no real means of consolidating its
authority. Thomas Clap, rector of Yale College, charged that some
persons in a congregation intentionally tried to blacken a minister's
reputation to get him dismissed. But perhaps the most common
weapon used by a community to rid itself of a minister with whom
it had grown disaffected was to withhold payment of his salary. Towns
throughout New England fell behind in paying their ministers' salaries,

while inflation seriously undercut the value of a minister's income, forcing him frequently to turn to the townspeople for a raise. Between 1680 and 1740, 12 percent of the ministers in New England and northern Long Island became entangled in financial disputes with their congregations, and 5 percent of these stepped down from their pulpits because of their problems in obtaining adequate financial support.

The Reverend Hugh Adams (HC 1697) requested dismissal from his pulpit in Braintree, Massachusetts, in 1710, complaining that the people there "Prov'd so Ungratefully Stubborn as to Deny" him "a competent and seasonable salary, and nothing at all for Settlement." Soon after assuming the ministry in Durham, New Hampshire, his relations with his parish were again problematical. Adams petitioned the provincial government to establish a statute like that of Massachusetts, which made the failure to pay a minister's salary a penal offence. He believed that Massachusetts's enactment of this statute had "proportionably spared [them] from the *throat Pestilence* and other impoverishing." During his lifetime, Adams changed pulpits seven times, mainly because, he explained, his parishioners refused to pay the salary they had promised him. Such high mobility, much like that of the poorly-trained New England empirics, must be seen as a sign of repeated failure to attain a satisfactory relationship with his parishioners. To compensate for his financial difficulties, Adams found that, through his "Occasional Practice of Physick and Chyrurgery for about 22 years past, The LORD hath included the hearts and hands of some of my Patients, so honestly & honourably to Reward my Cures, as to be so far maintained with such food and rayment hitherto as I and my family have been favour'd withall."[35] Only through the practice of medicine and surgery, claimed Adams, could he make a decent living, compensating for his consistent failure to secure an adequate clerical salary.

While ministers in New England found it more and more difficult to collect their full salaries, Harvard-trained ministers who had removed to England during the eighteenth century complained of similar problems. In 1718, the Reverend Rowland Cotton (HC 1696) had thoughts of returning to New England from Warminster, Wiltshire, which he described as a loose profane and horridly wicked part of the Earth. . . . we Dissenters in England have not Parishes with fixed Sallary's as in New England. . . . They are indeed most of them poor and scarse give me one quarter what my family annually expend, but having taken a Dr Degree in Holland [University of Harderwyck, 1697], by the practice of Physick, together with my wifes portion . . . I have acquir'd a competent substance.[36]

Obviously Cotton was out of touch with the struggles of his brethren in New England, and if he had returned there, more than likely he would have been forced to combine the two professions again to increase his income.

In 1691, the colonists reluctantly complied with the Crown's decree that "forever hereafter there shall be a Liberty of Conscience allowed in the Worship of God" in the Provinces of New England. No longer could the saints struggle to create an exclusive religious community. They were forced to embrace a variety of religions and give up the founders' ideal of the Holy Commonwealth in which church and state would be united by biblical morality. Yet by this time, many communities already had found it impossible to maintain the ideals of the Congregational Way, with only "visible saints" admitted to full church membership and the Lord's Supper. Many churches began to allow Christians professing faith the privileges of church membership, without publicly examining the candidate for proof of "saving faith." As Edmund S. Morgan explains, "In their different ways New Englanders tempered their zeal and adjusted their churches to a more worldly purity." The desire to establish purity in the churches may have dwindled, but it did not disappear, as men like Solomon Stoddard stirred zealotry by frightening sinners with visions of the tortures of hell. Hellfire preaching spread throughout England and the colonies, announcing the onset of the religious revival known as the Great Awakening. Following the lead of Jonathan Edwards, many New Englanders grew inspired with a new-found religious fervor and a desire for purity in their churches. Unprecedented turmoil in many congregations led to a splintering between the New Lights (who embraced the fervor of the revival), and the Old Lights (who favored a more liberal form of church government). With the mounting factionalism, many

groups completely broke away from their churches and started new
ones, or else, in an attempt to force a minister to step down from a
pulpit, intentionally "starved" ministers whose theological views differed from their own.[37]

As a result of this social disruption, the clergy found it nearly impossible to secure a peaceful and continuous pastorate; many clerics
were dismissed and forced to travel in search of another pulpit (see
groups 4, 5, and 6 in table 2.2). During these schismatic years of the
Awakening, the ministry became an increasingly unstable profession,
one whose members were forced to seek other means of gaining an
income. Naturally, many ministers were able to rely upon their medical skills after experiencing dismissal; or, if they were unable to collect
their full salaries from a faction-ridden congregation, many combined
the two professions as in earlier generations. Yet some congregations
grew critical of their ministers' involvement in a wordly profession.
Benjamin Doolittle's (YC 1716) congregation of Northfield sought his
dismissal "on account of his engrossing and widely extended medical
practice." In addition, there were doctrinal objections to his ministry
"on the score of Arminianism" (a belief that men by their own will-
power could achieve faith and therefore attain salvation), which was
perhaps the underlying reason that a faction had pressed for his dismissal. The Episcopal clergyman Isaac Browne (YC 1729) was transferred to a congregation in Newark in 1747 at a salary of fifty pounds
a year, but he outraged his parish by the medical fees he charged for
his services. In 1768 he was transferred to Perth Amboy because of
difficulties in Newark, but his new congregation refused to accept
him, stating that "his medical practice had been a fruitful source of
contention with his parishioners through the bills rendered by him
in that capacity."[38]

Samuel Bacheller (HC 1731), a preacher of the word at Haverhill,
Massachusetts, was charged with "preaching false doctrines" by a council of nine neighboring churches. He had caused much confusion
within his church by first taking the side of the New Lights and later
vehemently rejecting them, forcing those who embraced the Great
Awakening to withdraw from his ministry. His parishioners made a
number of charges against him, telling him, "You have spent much

of your time practising physick, and in farming business, . . . and on the Lord's day . . . entertain your people reading over old sermons." He was also accused of "managing" and perhaps causing a number of lawsuits. His parishioners condemned his worldliness and his neglect of the townspeople, claiming he had not visited some of them

Table 2.2

Number of Pulpits Held By Preacher-Physicians
(Percent)

(N=1265) Group No.	Not Available	0*	1	2	3 or More
1 (1630–1650) N=14	0.00	6.25	50.00	37.50	6.25
**2 (1651–1670) N=12	0.00	16.67	75.00	8.33	0.00
3 (1671–1690) N=11	9.09	0.00	81.82	9.09	0.00
4 (1691–1710) N=15	6.67	0.00	53.33	20.00	20.00
5 (1711–1730) N=23	9.09	13.64	45.45	18.18	13.64
6 (1731–1750) N=29	0.00	27.59	41.38	17.24	10.34
7 (1751–1770) N=22	14.29	23.81	38.10	9.52	14.29

*Individuals who were itinerants, as well as those who preached at various towns but were never ordained. **Figures for Groups 2–7 are somewhat skewed, since 25 to 33 percent of these individuals quit the ministry altogether. Although Groups 2 and 3 show a high percentage of ministers in secure positions of only one pulpit during their lifetime, remember that many others left the profession.

for twenty years. Even Bacheller's medical abilities were attacked when Elizabeth Currier testified that he was responsible for the death of a local woman's infant, a result of his assistance in the delivery of her baby (see chapter 5). The council concluded that when ministers engaged in secular business which interfered with the work of the ministry, it was "greatly criminal in them that watch for souls." Samuel Wigglesworth, another minister-physician, was a member of the council and not entirely unsympathetic to Bacheller's position. The council claimed that "a people should so support their pastor, as that he may not be under obligation . . . to engage in worldly incumbrances." But members of his parish replied that Bacheller had made a substantial fortune by engaging in "worldly business," thereby enriching his estate by several thousand pounds. They deemed him a criminal for neglecting the "work of the gospel to enrich his estate," and he then begrudgingly accepted dismissal.[39]

Although the people of New England had grown more worldly and more materialistic, many Congregational churches still expected their ministers to "gladly spend and be spent" for their communities. Yet as ministerial salaries failed to keep pace with rising inflation, which grew particularly severe during the successive military campaigns against the French and Indians in the eighteenth century, more and more ministers resorted to additional occupations such as medicine, law, farming, land speculation, and trade – a practice which frequently met with the disapproval of the community. Thomas Symmes (HC 1698) summarized the clergy's view of the dilemma succinctly at an ordination sermon of 1721, claiming that "a scandalous, or, (I had almost said) a scanty Maintenance, that obliges Ministers to neglect their Studies . . . or constrains them to do things beneath the Dignity of their Post, will surely produce a scandalous Ministry." The blame, he felt, rested squarely on the shoulders of the community. If only the parishioners would contribute "liberally and chearfully to their honourable subsistence," such a scandal surely could be avoided.[40]

While some communities grew hostile over the minister's extensive and costly medical practice, as well as his involvement in other capital-producing occupations, some communities actively encouraged their pastors to seek other means of bringing in income, because they felt unable to provide him with an adequate salary. The New Light minister Jacob Green (HC 1744) was encouraged to practice medicine by his parishioners because the only salary they could provide was quite low. His rural congregation felt that it simply could not have a minister unless he took some other initiative to help support his family and voted that "Mr. Green practice physick, if he can bair it and the presbytery approve it." Not only did Green practice medicine for pay, but he also became a land speculator and ran a gristmill.[41]

Perhaps some ministers were more successful in securing their promised salary from their parishioners because they acted as both minister and physician, which may have made them more valuable to the community. And perhaps, as a means of quieting the "outgroup"—those members of the community who were outside the church and who often complained bitterly about being forced to pay for the minister's maintenance—some divines provided medical services to the entire community free of charge as part of their evangelical pastoral responsibilities. The Reverend Henry Lucas claimed that "my little Knowledge in Physick has given me a great op[por]tunity of conversing with Men by which I have done that which by preaching I could not have done and by it I have saved our People more Money than ere they proposed to allow [me for a salary] and have not taken any thing for all I have done."[42]

Many ministers had grown reluctant to displease their people, for fear that they would withhold their salaries. "Ministers may be under Temptations," explained Azariah Mather to a young minister, "to go too far in seeking to Please the People, least they shut their Liberal Hands and close their Purse Strings." Unlike many of his colleagues during the Great Awakening, Thomas Smith (HC 1720) was minister to a single congregation during his entire lifetime. When other communities were deliberately withholding their parson's pay in these turbulent times, his Falmouth congregation regularly raised his salary, in part because he provided free medical care to his community. "I am hurried perpetually with the sick," he entered in his diary in 1748, "the whole practice rests on me, and God gives me reputation with satisfaction of mind, as being a successful instrument in his hands." In addition, Smith practiced during the dreadful epidemics of the throat distemper, with "hardly any escaping."[43] No doubt this factor made his services even more appreciated in a community that lacked a regular physician. Perhaps the unhealthiness of a particular region contributed to a town's belief that the medical minister was an extremely valuable and appreciated member of the community, especially when he practiced free of charge.

Although Congregational ministers throughout the colonial period often complained bitterly about their inability to collect their full salaries, they still enjoyed a relatively high degree of wealth and social status. Throughout the seventeenth century, ministers typically ranked at the top or just below it in town tax or population listings. On the eve of the American Revolution, free adult wealth-holders in New England had the lowest levels of per-capita income and wealth in mainland British America, with an average level of physical wealth estimated at 161 pounds. The clergy (as part of the category of professionals which included doctors and lawyers) ranked just below the merchant class and "esquires, gentlemen and officials," with a mean value of physical wealth rated at 270 pounds. New England communities grew increasingly resentful of their ministers, who they believed enjoyed significant wealth and status and who nevertheless relentlessly argued that they were underpaid.[44] This set of circumstances clearly paralleled that of England after the Protestant Reformation, when anticlericalism was rooted partly in the observation that the clergy enjoyed a separate and often more comfortable lifestyle.

Naturally, a minister's involvement in the healing arts or other income-producing occupations could raise his level of physical wealth. Available estate inventories (roughly one-third) of a group of twenty-nine minister-physicians who died during the Revolutionary era revealed an average level of physical wealth of 716 pounds, about 450 pounds higher than that of the average clergyman or doctor of the same time period. Although considerably more research needs to be done to determine the average levels of wealth of regular ministers and physicians compared to those of the minister-physicians over the entire colonial period, the preliminary figures in table 2.3 suggest that, by 1700, minister-physicians had accumulated higher levels of wealth than their counterparts in divinity and medicine. While it is difficult

Table 2.3
Average Amount of Preacher-Physicians' Estates at Death
(In Pounds)

Group No.	Number of Minister-Physicians	Average Estate	Number of Regular Ministers	Average Estate	Number of Regular Physicians	Average Estate
1 (1630–1650)	5	975	1	1,239	1	6
2 (1651–1670)	3	757	5	945	2	70
3 (1671–1690)	1	4,257	1	1,501	0	–
4 (1691–1710)	8	2,344	6	1,366	3	114
5 (1711–1730)	7	3,603	8	1,773	3	1,125
6 (1731–1750)	10	1,743	10	1,165	12	1,535
7 (1751–1770)	4	1,589	4	1,051	0	–

to determine the actual amount of wealth generated from medical practice, it is perhaps safe to suggest that clerical medical practice could often be a means of generating substantial wealth for some ministers.

By the middle decades of the eighteenth century, the power of Puritan social institutions had diminished considerably. As New Englanders increasingly demanded more liberty for themselves and less power for the authorities (including the clergy), they also labored tenaciously to increase their material wealth.[45] Even ministers often exhibited a profound desire to increase their wealth, amassing property or engaging in trade. Christopher Toppan (HC 1691) was a minister, physician, and surgeon, as well as a land speculator who became involved in legal disputes over his various holdings. John Tucke (HC 1723) acted as minister, physician, teacher, and storekeeper; and Solomon Stoddard's son Anthony (HC 1697) was minister, physician, the town lawyer, the judge of probate, and he also had one of the largest farms in the region. A minister's "conversion" from Puritan to Yankee typically enraged the public, which sought to sustain clergymen in their mythical seventeenth-century character as otherworldly preachers of the word. Although Puritanism has not been characterized as an ascetic religion, Michael Walzer argues that it was "hardly an ideology which encouraged continuous or unrestrained accumulation. Instead, the saints tended to be narrow and conservative in their need for a modest life, or, alternatively, to use up their surplus in charitable giving. . . . Unremitting and relatively unremunerative work was the greatest help toward saintliness and virtue." By 1765, the pursuit of "selfish gain" had grown more acceptable.[46] The minister, however, still was expected to "spend and be spent" for the community.

At the founding of New England, first-generation ministers who had immigrated often had learned medicine as a second occupation, first, because of rampant religious persecution of Puritans in the mother country and, second, to bolster often appallingly low clerical salaries. Once in New England, the manner of establishing Congregational churches was slow and cautious. So the minister hopeful of settlement in a particular community had to rely on other means to support himself. Given the church's long association with the healing arts, many candidates naturally fell back upon medicine while awaiting ordination. In addition, many early New England communities were impoverished and thus were unable (and unwilling) to give the minister adequate support. Therefore many ministers continued to practice medicine even after settlement, in order to raise their standards of living. After all, the clergy were college-educated, "the more learned the better,"[47] and often the only individuals with such a level of education in their communities, especially in rural areas. Thus they had a social position to uphold in the community, and social status reflected not only a man's occupation but also his level of material wealth. In addition, ministers experienced a profound increase in status after immigrating, placing new pressures on them to maintain their elevated status within the community. Perhaps many ministers worked two jobs in part to maintain a particular social standing.

In subsequent generations, New England's communities grew increasingly contentious over such matters as the structure of the church, eligibility requirements for church membership and baptism, and even such seemingly insignificant matters as whether or not the congregation should sing or chant hymns. This tension between the members of the church and the community at large and between the minister and his flock revealed a crisis in the minister's authority in the community. Churches increasingly dismissed one minister and hired another over a variety of issues, making the ministry a decreasingly attractive career choice for graduates of Yale and Harvard. Aware of the problems within many New England churches, particularly after the end of the seventeenth century, ministers continued to learn the art of medicine as a second occupation in case their first choice, divinity, proved to be untenable. The uncertain situation in New England, particularly during the decades of the Great Awakening, when congregations were intentionally attempting to "starve" their ministers by withholding pay, greatly resembled the atmosphere of England when the first generations migrated to the New World. This pattern of uncertainty had recurred, and ministers responded shrewdly by diversifying their knowledge and skills. They learned the art of medicine as their Puritan forefathers had done before them, as a means of leaving one job market for a more secure one. Only the first generation of immigrant clergy almost uniformly remained in the ministry, while nearly a third of all subsequent colonial generations of minister-physicians gave up a career in the church for a less problematical and more worldly one in medicine (see table 2.4). In addition, from the early eighteenth century to the Revolution, fewer and fewer graduates of Harvard and Yale chose the dual path of the minister-physician. Particularly around the middle of the eighteenth century, an increasing number of Harvard and Yale graduates chose the profes-

Table 2.4
Preacher-Physicians Who Remained In or Quit the Ministry

(N=126) Group No.	Not Available (Percent)	Remained (Percent)	Quit (Percent)
1 (1630–1650) N=14	0.00	93.75	6.25
2 (1651–1670) N=12	0.00	66.67	33.33
3 (1671–1690) N=11	9.09	63.64	27.27
4 (1691–1710) N=15	6.67	60.00	33.33
5 (1711–1730) N=23	4.55	72.73	22.72
6 (1731–1750) N=29	0.00	65.52	34.48
7 (1751–1770) N=22	4.76	71.43	23.81

Table 2.5
Yale Graduates

Class Years	Total Number Students	Total Number Physicians	Physicians (Percent)	Total Number Minister-Physicians	(Percent)
1704–1710	31	1	3.3	3	9.7
1711–1720	55	0	0.0	5	9.1
1721–1730	140	9	6.4	6	4.3
1731–1740	179	13	7.3	2	1.1
1741–1750	153	18	11.8	5	3.3
1751–1760	290	28	9.7	7	2.4
1761–1770	322	39	12.1	4	1.2

Table 2.6
Harvard Graduates

Class Years	Total Number Students	Total Number Physicians	Physicians (Percent)	Total Number Minister–Physicians	(Percent)
1704–1710	86	12	14.0	6	7.0
1711–1720	168	14	8.3	5	3.0
1721–1730	388	51	13.1	20	5.2
1731–1740	340	41	12.1	16	4.7
1741–1750	268	35	13.1	4	1.5
1751–1760	299	39	13.0	9	3.0
1761–1770	534	88	16.5	6	1.1

Table 2.7
Yale and Harvard Graduates

Class Years	Total Number Students	Total Number Physicians	Physicians (Percent)	Total Number Minister-Physicians	(Percent)
1704–1710	117	13	11.1	9	7.7
1711–1720	223	14	6.3	10	4.5
1721–1730	528	60	11.4	26	4.9
1731–1740	519	54	10.4	18	3.5
1741–1750	421	53	12.6	9	2.1
1751–1760	589	67	11.4	16	2.7
1761–1770	856	127	14.8	10	1.2

sion of medicine directly upon graduation (see tables 2.5, 2.6, and 2.7). This pattern of career choice reflects the many changes which occurred in New England society during the eighteenth century and underscores the emergence of a modern, diversified, secular society.

Although the clergy were "holy" men engaged in a spiritual occupation, they were still professionals seeking stable, secure employment. This fact is crucial in understanding the widespread phenomenon of the angelical conjunction in New England, which resulted from the confluence of a number of factors other than the motive of providing health care out of Christian charity. Viewed within the context of the emergence of New England as a modern capitalistic society, the preacher-physician often was a protean and intuitive tactician, very much in touch with society's changing moods.

Chapter 3

Galen's Legacy

The first generation of Puritan ministers who settled in New England often came to the New World armed with a knowledge of medical theories and remedies to treat the sick in their communities. As in the English provinces they left behind, in the colonies there was no effective governing body to control the standards of medical care, and the general practitioner who compounded his own drugs typified the cleric's role as healer. Having explored various factors that stimulated the proliferation of the minister-physician in New England, in the following three chapters I will examine: (1) the minister-physicians' understanding of the "secondary" or natural causes of disease; (2) the quality of medical care they provided; (3) the ways in which their understanding of medicine and surgery deviated from or replicated English models; and (4) the differences and similarities between clerical medical practices, those of regular physicians, and the folk remedies of the laity.

Two schools of thought influenced clerical and regular medical practice in New England during the first century of settlement: the Galenic-humoral and the Paracelsian-iatrochemical. Galen was a Greek physician who flourished in the second century A.D. His medical theories, based on the quality and balance of the four bodily humors (blood, phlegm, black bile, and yellow bile), dominated medical practice until the time of Vesalius. Galenic theory continued to influence lay and professional medical knowledge and practice until well into the nineteenth century. During the sixteenth century, as opposition to scholasticism mounted, the Swiss physician Paracelsus rejected Galenism and developed a medical system which, based on chemistry, promoted an ontological concept of disease.[1]

This chapter addresses the influence of Galenic humoral theory on clerical thought and medical practice in colonial New England, focusing upon the contents of the medical works ministers collected for their libraries. Clerical collections of remedies, as well as relevant letters and diaries, have been examined for evidence of Galenic influence and the findings assessed in light of popular attitudes towards healing. In many herbals and almanacs of the period, such popular subjects as the role of astrology in medical practice were integrally linked to humoral theory. Clerical attitudes towards these occult aspects of medical practice will be explored. In addition, the poetry and sermons of a sample of the ministers in this study are examined to determine whether or not Galenic humoral theory influenced Puritan modes of religious expression.

An analysis of nearly one-third of the estate inventories of the ministers in this study, in addition to their published library lists, has yielded itemized contents of nineteen libraries (approximately half of the inventories surveyed had a library).[2] While the sizes of their libraries varied, the ministers collected many of the same medical authors (see table 3.1). The most popular medical authority among this group was the astrological physician Nicholas Culpeper (1616–54). The son of a clergyman, Culpeper was an ardent Puritan who spent some time at Cambridge, where he learned Latin and Greek, became apprenticed to an apothecary, and finally started his own medical practice. Nearly half of the clerical libraries surveyed contained one or more works by Culpeper, generally either his *Pharmacopoeia Londinensis; or the London Dispensatory* (London, 1653) or his most famous publication, *The English Physician* (London, 1652), which became known as "Culpeper's Herbal." Over one-quarter of the libraries surveyed also contained the herbals of William Salmon (1644–1713), the English empiric.[3] The works of both Culpeper and Salmon typically contain alphabetical lists of herbs or ailments whose curative powers are explained according to traditional Galenic humoral theory. Interspersed throughout are astrological hints for the proper procurement and preparation of remedies. Both Culpeper and Salmon adhered to the widespread belief that local plants contained an abundance of healing properties, and that the use of exotic (and costly) herbs by academic physicians was a deplorable practice. Culpeper once had a stirring vision in which "All the sick People in England presented themselves

Table 3.1
Medical Authorities Most Popular Among Preacher-Physicians

Owner of Library	Bartholin	Boerhaave	Cooke	Croll	Culpeper	Descartes	Fernel	Harvey	Van Helmont	Hippocrates	Occult/Magic	Quincy	Riverius	Salmon	Schroeder	Sennert	Turner	Willis
Samuel Lee (1625–1691)	•			•		•	•	•	•	•	•		•		•	•		•
Leonard Hoar (1630–1675)	•								•	•	•							
Michael Wigglesworth (1631–1705)				•	•			•					•			•		•
Gershom Bulkeley (c. 1636–1713)	•		•	•	•		•		•	•	•		•	•	•	•		•
Edward Taylor (1642–1729)					•										•			
Israel Chauncy (1644–1709)											•				•			
Samuel Brackenbury (1646–1678)	•		•	•	•	•			•				•			•		

	William Brattle (1662–1717)	Cotton Mather (1663–1728)	Phineas Fiske (1682–1738)	Elisha Mix (1705–1739)	Dudley Woodbridge (1705–1790)	John Williams (1706–1774)	Moses Bartlett (1708–1766)	Timothy Mix (1711–1779)	Joseph Lamson (1718–1773)	Eneas Munson (1734–1826)	Nathaniel Hooker (1737–1770)	Jonathan Bird (1747–1813)
	•								•			
			•									
	•							•				
	•		•									
					•		•	•			•	•
		•	•									
											•	
		•	•									
		•	•									
	•						•	•	•		•	
			•									
		•	•		•				•	•		
		•	•									

before me, and told They had Herbes in thier Gardens that might cure them, but knew not the vertues of them."[4]

The herbal was the mainstay of popular medical practice in both England and the colonies of New England throughout the colonial period. An examination of the contents of the libraries of fifteen New England physicians, contemporary Boston booksellers' lists, and lay libraries of the period indicates that Culpeper's herbals were the most popular medical works in all of Puritan New England. A third of the physicians' libraries (85 percent of which were eighteenth-century collections) contained works by Culpeper.[5] And women, who usually took on the role of healer in the home, also were known to possess their own copies of Culpeper, and his works were often passed down from mother to daughter. For example, Culpeper's *Pharmacopoeia Londinensis* (London, 1667 edition) was owned by Elizabeth Greenleaf, wife of the parson-physician Daniel Greenleaf (HC 1696), who opened her own apothecary shop in Boston. She passed her Culpeper down to her daughter Grace in 1764, and two years later Grace presented her sister with the same volume.[6]

Certainly one of the aspects of the Culpeper and Salmon dispensatories most attractive to New England Puritans was the strong revolutionary tone of the works, which condemned Anglican attempts to control the government, the church, and the professions. Culpeper demanded the "Liberty of the Subject" from the tyranny of "Priests, Physitians, Lawyers." Puritan social reformers such as Culpeper connected the monopolistic tendencies of these three professions and denounced them because, they claimed, clerics extorted tithes from their parishes, lawyers robbed the public of legal fees, and physicians charged exhorbitant fees and perpetuated rather than ameliorated illness and suffering. Comparing the medical elite of the Royal College of Physicians (incorporated in 1518) to the Papists who refused to allow the vernacular printing of theological materials, Culpeper condemned medical attempts to conceal knowledge in the Latin tongue. He produced a number of extremely popular medical manuals in the vernacular to provide the reading public with the "secrets" of physick, enabling many individuals to earn an income as healers.[7]

During the interregnum, when censorship and medical licensing were suspended, England experienced a virtual explosion in the publication of medical works in the vernacular. The New England colonists certainly profited by the suspension, as a greater variety of books became available to them. Vernacular medical literature had been published during the Laudian period and on an even more limited scale during the sixteenth century; however, reprints of popular collections of recipes had dominated the publishing scene, with only a few original works. Now a number of authors and translators began to flood the market with vernacular medical treatises, particularly during the 1650s; their publications often were prompted by an ideological commitment to the Puritan social reform movement. Culpeper, certainly one of the most prolific authors of this genre, launched his attack on the monopolistic College of Physicians by producing an unauthorized translation of their *Pharmacopoeia* (London, 1618), a compendium of Galenic herbal remedies. The translation from Latin into English was published in 1649 under the title, A *Physicall Directory, or a Translation of the London Dispensatory*. Although Culpeper did follow the original *Pharmacopoeia* rather closely, he freely added his own commentary, inserted more chemical remedies, and was not above occasionally slandering the college's reputation.[8] It is hardly surprising that Culpeper's writings (as well as those of Salmon), so firmly entrenched in the antiroyalist, antimonopolistic polemic of his day, were so popular among the Puritan ministers of New England.

It was quite common for the New England minister to put together his own personal collection of medical remedies which he called his "dispensatory" or "*vade mecum*." He would copy herbal "recipes" from Culpeper and Salmon, as well as from other medical authorities, which were to be administered according to Galenic humoral theory. In his dispensatory of 1696 (intended for his own private use), the Reverend Thomas Palmer of Middleborough, Massachusetts, explained that it was necessary for the healer to follow basic Galenic principles when called to the sickbed of a parishioner: the first thing he should do is "consider whether it [the illness] be a humoural Distemper & what Humours are most afflictive, & what parts of the body are most distempered, & where the seat of the disease lyes." He then chose from an arsenal of remedies he had collected, of which "there be sundry kinds. Some work chiefly by Vomit [emetics], some cheifly do work downward [purgatives], some work both *ways*; some are Violent & dangerous. . . . Others are . . . safe. . . . Some purge Phlegm, some choler [yellow bile], some Melancholy [black bile], some most humours, & some all humours." It was essential for the healer to take into account the "age, strength, custom of the patient, season & manner of ordering," and administer cures "sutable to the nature of the humor" afflicted, or else he could jeopardize the patient's life.[9]

In the Galenic system, the four primary elements were earth, air, fire, and water. These came into existence through a combination of the four primary qualities: hot, dry, wet, and cold. The qualities related to the elements in pairs, thus water was cold and wet, fire was hot and dry, air was hot and wet, and earth was cold and dry. The elements and qualities related to the four bodily humors: blood, phlegm, yellow bile, and black bile, which were derived from the food eaten. The humors received their characteristic properties in the liver and were carried by the veins to the solid parts of the body. Galenists believed that blood, phlegm, yellow bile, and black bile predominated in the heart, brain, liver, and spleen respectively. The four human "temperaments," known as sanguine, phlegmatic, choleric, and melancholic, were a result of the particular combination of qualities and humors within the individual. When an imbalance between the humors and the qualities occurred, equilibrium could be restored by administering therapies associated with the opposite qualities, with the patient's individual temperament always kept in mind. As Culpeper explained, "all Diseases are cured by their contraries, but all parts of the Body maintained by their likes. Then if the heat be the cause of the disease, give cold Medicine appropriated to it."[10]

Although the minister could resort to the use of chemical or mineral preparations to restore the humoral balance (see chapter 4), he typically chose a "simple," which was composed of a single herbal ingredient, according to its appropriate degree of heat, coolness, wetness, or dryness; or a "compound," a mixture of two or more simples. For example, in describing the value of fennel, Culpeper informs his readers that "the Root is hot and dry, some say in the third degree, opening; it provokes Urine, and the terms [menses]; strengthens the Liver, and is good against the Dropsie."[11]

In addition to extracting remedies from the popular herbals in the creation of his dispensatory, the minister also collected recipes from other ministers skilled in medicine, physicians, family members, and his own parishioners. The Reverend Edward Taylor (HC 1671), the frontier parson of Westborough, Massachusetts, even stooped so low as to collect remedies from a neighboring Jesuit priest. Like the Galenic treatments recommended in the popular pharmacopoeias of Culpeper and Salmon, most of the remedies exchanged in this network called for healing plants, roots, and barks, in addition to common household items such as raisins, honey, and wine. For example, the Reverend Jared Eliot (YC 1706) sent a fellow minister a recipe for a "Catarrhous humour" which consisted of a plant which was a popular emetic, ipecac, together with the garden herb camomile, "steeped in wine . . . [with] the yoke of an egg in cyder sweetened with honey." From "Sister Blower" the Reverend Thomas Symmes (HC 1698) obtained several "Receipts for Worms in Children" (a common problem in colonial New England) which contained garlic, eggs, and rye.[12] One may gather from the list of often unsavory ingredients and procedures in many recipes that some of the cures administered by the ministry must have been quite unpleasant to the patient. For example, from Peter Tolman of Guilford, Connecticut, the Reverend Gershom Bulkeley obtained a cure for the "dropsie," which called for "making highe incisions in ye swollen legs" and then "applying all over ye legs a pultisse [poultice] made of Indian meal boiled w[it]h Mullen leaves, w[hi]ch drawes out ye water." And in order to make a "most healing, Knitting Plaister, boil Green comf[r]ey roots pounded soft, with which mix Angle worms, not pounded," recommended the Reverend Ezra Carpenter (HC 1720).[13]

As the records of Rev. Bulkeley indicate, remedies often were obtained at second or third hand, depending on the reputed success of a particular concoction. He procured one remedy for the "Wind Collicke" which was "sent by (my now father in Law) Mr. Charles Chauncey [former Harvard president and also a minister-physician] then of Situate, May 3, 1648, to my own father Mr. Peter Bulkeley [also a min-ister] of Concord." The remedy consisted of toasted bread, soaked in wine and applied hot to the navel, which was believed to draw out the offending humor much as the bread soaked up the wine. Bulkeley also obtained from one Mr. Bradstreete of New London, a remedy formulated by the Reverend Thomas Thacher, the author of New England's first published medical treatise. Thus it appears that the clergy went to great lengths to appropriate remedies, often from other ministers with reputations as famous healers.[14]

This remedy-exchange network also functioned among the laity, as surviving collections demonstrate. A carpenter in Brookline, Mas-sachusetts, Timothy Harris (1650–1730), put together his own dis-pensatory composed of recipes gathered from various acquaintances. Claims about the effectiveness of certain remedies were obviously exaggerated, as one concoction from Joshua Child was deemed "good against the mezels poks plage spoted fever and all malignishall Dezes-ses malignisticall desesses." Carpenter obviously took some liberties in his spelling. Like many of the simpler remedies of the clergy, those of the laity mainly consisted of household items such as raisins and wine mixed with garden herbs.[15]

From Timothy Briant in his hometown of Middleborough, the Reverend Ebenezer Parkman received a detailed set of instructions and remedies for the treatment of the "Throat Distemper," which was probably diphtheria (or a combination of diphtheria and scarlet fever). At various periods over the course of the eighteenth century, diph-theria, the grim reaper of children, raged in epidemic form in many regions of New England. It was considered a new and unusual illness, "vastly beyond whatever has been known in these parts before," Briant wrote to Parkman. Many clerical remedy collections from this period naturally contain one or more remedies for this virulent, contagious disease. The widespread remedy network that existed throughout New England in the colonial era was particularly responsive to the need to keep in check epidemics such as the throat distemper. And often the remedies which these ministers collected were tailored to the species of healing plants which were available in a given region. Parker's recipe from Timothy Briant was composed of "Plaintain,

Sassaparilla, Blood-wort and Canker-root . . . such as commonly grows about your Door or Barn. . . . these means are easy for comon People to get." Ministers like Parkman also copied remedies from newspapers such as the *Boston Evening Post* and the *Massachusetts Gazette* and journals such as the *Universal Magazine*. Local newspapers also responded to crises like these, publishing remedies from various sources. Parkman copied a selection from the *Boston Evening Post* of 20 November 1769 prescribing treatment of the throat distemper; the author had provided his cure "being moved with Compassion for ye distressed Condition of ye p[eo]p[le] in Boston & Oxford."[16]

In *The Countrey Parson* (1633), George Herbert extols the virtues of common garden herbs for use during the parson's visitation of the sick. The simplicity and beauty of medicinal plants displayed "the manifold wisdom of God," he explained, and it was necessary for the parson "to know what herbs may be used" in place of costly and exotic drugs: "For home-bred medicines are both more easie for the Parson's purse, and more familiar for all mens bodyes. So, where the Apothecary useth either for loosing [purging], Rhubarb, or for binding, Bolearmena, the Parson useth damask or white Roses for the one, and plantaine, sheperds purse, knotgrasse for the other, and that with better successe." Nicholas Culpeper was also committed to providing inexpensive remedies for the poor, both through his publications and in his own medical practice. His *Medicaments for the Poor, or Physick for the Common People* (1656) was composed chiefly of easily accessible garden herbs. The Reverend Edward Taylor's name is inscribed in a 1670 edition of this work, and even the alchemical physician Gershom Bulkeley copied remedies from the Culpeper edition which called for such common household items as oatmeal, vinegar, bran, and wine, as well as garden herbs.[17] The advantages of using common garden herbs were threefold: they were often perceived as more agreeable to the system, more readily available than exotic imports, and easier on the "purse."

Another commonly used form of Galenic therapy was phlebotomy or bloodletting. This was indicated "in abundance of blood & inflammation of blood," explained the Reverend Thomas Palmer. The clergy recognized that bloodletting was a risky procedure: "In some cases blood-letting saves life, and in some cases destroys it," Palmer continued. He recorded a case where he "once bled DC in the arm for the falling sickness [epilepsy] hoping it was the cure usually meant; it killed him." One historian of medicine has claimed that the New England ministry tended to "bleed and pray" in all severe cases. Although it is impossible to determine the frequency with which clerics bled their patients, colonial diaries and letters indicate that the ministry performed venesection with a fair degree of regularity.[18]

In addition to the personal clerical dispensatories and medical treatises that dappled the shelves of ministerial libraries, another rich body of writings reflects the influence of Galenic humoral theory on clerical medical thought and practice. The sermons and poetry of a number of the clergymen in my sample consistently employ medical metaphor, often Galenic in origin, to express religious themes. Michael Wigglesworth often relied upon Galenic allusion and metaphor in his critique of New England's apostasies. Wigglesworth, who owned a copy of Culpeper's *English Physician*, was thoroughly familiar with the tenets of Galenism and possessed a knowledge of herbal remedies that were thought to restore the body's humoral balance. He portrayed disease as God's powerful tool for subduing the colonists' sinful ways:

> Much Honey turns to Gall
> And Cholerick excess;
> And too-too-much Prosperity
> Breeds Pride and Wantonness:
> Afflictions purge them out,
> Like bitter Aloe,
> Which, though unpleasant to the taste,
> Far wholsomer may be
>
> Full Diet, dainty Fare
> With Idleness and Ease
> Heap up bad Humours, and contract
> Many a foul Disease,
> To Soul, and Body too,
> Dang'rous, and Troublesome;
> Which must be purged out in Time
> By some *Catholicum*.[19]

Gluttony, pride, worldliness, sloth – these were the sins which angered a judgmental God. The result was an excess of "bad Humours" like the yellow bile ("Cholerick excess") which corrupted both body and soul. The "foul Disease" was God's chastisement, which, it was hoped, would "purge" out sinfulness "like bitter Aloe," a purgative plant imported from the West Indies and widely used by New Englanders. George Herbert, using penetrating conceits, explains that "God . . . stabs the wicked, as an enemy, with his Sword: but lances the godly, as a Surgeon his Patient, with the Launcet," an instrument used for bloodletting. "Thus *chastisements* befall the godly," he explained, "but *punishments* the wicked." The severity of God's punishments reflected man's spiritual condition, and the godly were merely "lanced" as a warning to correct their backslidings. And just as "Physick" stirred up "ill humours," so "Corruptions may be stirr'd by chastisements."[20]

"Galenicals" such as aloe, which induced vomiting or purging, often found their way into the sermons and poems of these ministers, and the perceived pharmacological action associated with a given herb was described in order to heighten religious themes. Addressing schism within the Puritan congregations, the Reverend Giles Firmin (who is thought to have performed the first dissection of a human body for instructional purposes in the New England colonies) insisted that "congregations must be mended by degrees: to *purge per vices* in foule bodies, is better then at first to give *Hellebore, Scammony,* and such strong workers."[21] A physician as well as a minster, Firmin's mind naturally turned to Galenic notions of using a gentle purge to cleanse "foule bodies" of contentiousness. The use of radical measures to resolve dissension within a church, much like the use of powerful and poisonous purgatives like Hellebore, was, in Firmin's thinking, too harsh an approach.

America's preeminent colonial bard, the Reverend Edward Taylor, uses his poetry as a meditative vehicle for exploring the pathology of his own soul's "illnesses." He portrays Christ as the healer of sin-sick souls; Christ alone can purge the corrupt "Ill Humours" of man's depraved condition, much as a given herbal decoction was thought to purge away the overabundant or corrupt humor which generated sickness:

> The Blood Red Pretious Syrup of this Rose
>   Doth all Catholicons excell what ere.
> Ill Humours all that do the Soule inclose
>   When rightly used, it purgeth out most
>   clear.
>   Lord purge my Soul with this Choice Syrup
>   and
>   Chase all thine enemies out of my
>   land.[22]

Since ancient Greek times, philosophers had relied upon medical metaphor to symbolize the grievances and turmoil of the soul as bodily disease, and this pattern of expression proliferated throughout the rise of Christianity. In resorting to medical symbolism to describe the condition of man's soul, Puritan ministers of New England drew upon the precedent of the early church fathers as well as upon contemporary Puritan guides to spiritual regeneration. Thomas Fuller's *Holy State* (1642) characterizes William Perkins as the model Puritan preacher, "an excellent chirurgeon [surgeon] . . . at the jointing of a broken soul."[23]

To wash away the sins of mankind, Christians believed that Christ had offered his own blood, represented by the wine of Holy Communion. When the minister opened his patient's vein to release "corrupted" blood, a cleansing act analogous to the drinking of Holy Wine was performed, one which rid the body of physical rather than spiritual impurities. George Herbert characterized the drinking of Holy Wine as a "comfortable, and Soveraigne . . . Medicine . . . to all sin-Sick souls." Wigglesworth also drew such an analogy in his best-selling poem, *Meat out of the Eater* (1670):

> Unto the cleansing Blood
>   Of Jesus Christ he flies;
> And to his wounded Conscience
>   That Soveraign Balm applies;
>   Which can both cleanse and heal;
>   Both pacifie God's wrath,
> And cure a guilty sin-sick Soul,
>   When 'tis improv'd by Faith.[24]

The Reverend Charles Chauncy, bemoaning man's fallen spiritual condition, warned his readers that "nothing less than the *blood of God* could redeem us. . . . We are drinking in the Wine, and strong Drink, while God is letting out our Blood."[25] Here Chauncy appears to suggest that man's corrupt ways would lead to God's chastisement through the scourge of disease, necessitating the "letting out" of blood in Galenic fashion to bring about a cure. Although the practice of bloodletting dates back to the time of Hippocrates, with the rise of Christianity, phlebotomy may have taken on a religious aura: as Christ "gave his blood" to redeem mankind of his sins, so man's blood becomes "corrupt" in many illnesses, and he must "give blood" like Christ did in order to purify the body and restore the balance of the four humors.

For many of these Puritan ministers who also practiced medicine upon their parishioners, the language of pathology was also the language of theology. The preacher-physician tried both to relieve the grieved and tortured consciences of his flock and to heal their sickly bodies. The dual nature of this professional path led these practitioners to see such religious themes as the condition of man's soul and the sacrament of the Lord's Supper in terms of medical modes of thinking, often based on Galenic humoralism. The contentiousness that plagued the churches of New England after the second half of the seventeenth century naturally was denounced in the jeremiads as a "disease" of society; paralleling society's "ills," ministers like Wigglesworth observed an actual increase in bodily disease. And, of course, the Puritan conviction of the interconnection of sin and disease made the minister's flock receptive to the powerful yet "plain" use of medical metaphor in the sermon. Although most Puritans probably were not skilled in the intricacies of Galenic physiology, they knew the basic tenets of the doctrine and, from their rich heritage of folk medicine, the uses of many herbs to purge common maladies; therefore the minister's medical metaphors did not fall on deaf ears. The clergy's use of Galenic metaphors was not a coincidental occurrence; rather, it reflected their medical knowledge as well as their belief in the relationship between man's body and soul. In reading Plato, Cotton Mather found him "eloquently demonstrating, That all *Diseases* have their Origin in the *Soul*." And in his advice to students of the cloth, *Manaductio ad Ministerium* (1726), Cotton Mather explained that disorders of the conscience could lead to physical disease. He urged the formation of a partnership between minister and physician to treat the two interrelated disorders.[26] But the minister who practiced medicine tried to heal the two types of disorders simultaneously on visits to sick parishioners, where he observed that a distressed conscience often accompanied life-threatening illness, as the thought of facing God's judgment after death threw many into the depths of despair.

In addition to Galenic influence in the herbals of Culpeper and Salmon, so prized by the clergy, in personal clerical dispensatories, and in medical metaphors in sermons and poetry, such occult concepts as the role of astrology in humoral medicine also were incorporated into both remedy collections and medical books collected by ministers. For example, in the preface to Culpeper's *Pharmacopoeia* is a note to the reader in which the author indicates his approach to the treatment of disease: "If thou ever intendest to study Physick," he wrote, "and turn neither Fool nor Knave in that famous Science, be well skilled in this Astrologo-Physical Discourse." He explained that "the Natural Faculty or Virtue resides in the Liver, and is generally governed by Jupiter. . . . From this are bred four particular Humors, Blood, Choler, Flegm, Melancholy." Culpeper's "Astrologo-Physical Discourse" contains references to astrologically correct times and methods of gathering and using herbs. Culpeper had established his practice as both physician and astrologer in 1640, and, at this time, astrology was widely accepted on both sides of the Atlantic, by the laity as well as by a number of reputable physicians. Even as late as 1724, Cotton Mather harshly denounced the widespread belief in astrology in New England. Mather viewed the role of astrology in medical practice as particularly deplorable: "The Assigning of particular *Plants* to particular *Planets*, or to say, as your *Culpepper* continually does, that such an Herb is governed by *Saturn* . . . and the Rest; It is a Folly akin to the Idolatry and the Superstition of the *Roman-Catholicks*, in looking to *Saints*, for their influences on our Several *Diseases*. Tis amazing to see Mankind so *Planet-Struck*.[27]

Nearly a third of the ministers' libraries surveyed in this study contained the Galenic treatises of Lazare Riviere, better known as Riverius (1589–1655). In discussing Galen's concept of the "critical days," that period of an illness when the disease crisis occurred, his *Institutiones Medicinae* (1655) provided crucial astrological information about the dominion of the moon over the body as it passed through the various zodiacal constellations in the heavens. The Reverend Gershom Bulkeley copied lengthy passages from the *Praxis Medicinae* (1660) of Riverius, from whom he learned that "peony gathered under its p[ro]p[er] constellation, viz. when the moon is descendent in the figure of Aries, doth remove of falling sickness [epilepsy], onely by externall application." The Reverend Thomas Palmer also consulted the works of Riverius and Culpeper in the preparation of his *vade mecum* of 1696, and he too considered the position of the moon in the heavens to be a crucial factor in determining the critical days and time of recovery: "If many good signs appear at the beginning of a fever, note the signe & degree the moon was in at the decumbiture & the party will recover when the moon comes to the sextile of the place she was then in." In other words, the patient would recover once the moon had passed through one-sixth of its circuit from the day the sick party took ill. Palmer also notes that the elderly are more susceptible to "quartane agues" than young people "because Saturn causes them."[28]

Obviously under the sway of Culpeper's "Astrologo-Physical Discourse," the frontier parson Edward Taylor, who owned three volumes of the works of Culpeper, entered a remedy into this personal dispensatory made of "Adders Tongue," which was used "to stop . . . bleeding at mouth, or nose, or inward wounds . . . [also for] inflamations caused by ye pains of hurts or wounds." This famed wound-healing plant "is under ye moons Domminion . . . & Saturnes" and, according to Taylor, was beneficial for "any Saturn Diseases."[29]

The commonplace book of the Reverend Ezra Carpenter was composed during the decades following his graduation from Harvard College in 1720, and, even at this late period in colonial history, astrology apparently guided his medical ministrations. At the beginning of his manuscript, he recorded: "For Bleeding/ Cancer is Indifferent/ Virgo Indiff[erent]/ Lib[r]a right good/ Scorp[io] Indiff[erent]/ Sagit[arius] good/ Aqua[rius] Indiff[erent]/ Pisces Indiff[erent]." The son of a farmer, Carpenter possessed agricultural expertise, no doubt passed down through the family, that also was guided by the heavens. He wrote that it was best to "Sow Hay Seed upon the Snow, then Mow over the Ground that same year 3 Times, in the Wane or Old of the Moon, the older Moon the better."[30]

Jean Calvin believed that physicians used their knowledge of the heavens properly when they selected suitable times for bleeding their patients or administering medicines, because, he claimed, there is "quelque convenance" between the luminaries and our bodies. However, like Martin Luther, he strongly opposed judicial or divinatory astrology as diabolical superstition. In Calvin's opinion, although *Genesis* claims that the lights were placed in the heavens as signs for mankind, he interprets the passage to mean that they are useful to farmers in guiding their planting and harvesting and to physicians in determining propitious times for bleeding and collecting herbs. Divinatory astrology, on the other hand, with the casting of nativities and the prediction of future events, he condemned as excessive and a challenge to the providence of God, who alone knew what the future held in store. The Puritan divine Charles Morton's *Compendium Physicae* was used as a physics text at Harvard from the 1680s through the 1720s, and, in this work, Morton, like Calvin, condemned judicial astrology but favored "natural astrology," the belief that the heavens influenced but did not control the events of the natural world.[31]

Regardless of Calvin's castigations, divinatory astrology was indeed practiced by at least two of the ministers in this study. The Reverend John Allin removed to England after graduating from Harvard College in the class of 1643, and there, away from the scrutiny of New England's more orthodox clerics, he practiced both medicine and astrology. With the arrival of the dreaded plague in 1665, Allin attempted to discover his own fate through the art as the epidemic raged:

> I am yet very well, though never without dayly feares . . . for Mars
> is comeing to my ascendant in my nativity, w[hic]h was there lord of
> the eighth; and in my revolution for this yeare Lord of the Asc[endant],
> and in his course of p[ro]gresse and regradation hee will continue within

the compasse of my ascecndant in my nativity till 1st July next. I had
thought to send Mr. Jeake the scheames with ye directions, and p[er]fec-
tions for this yeare for his judgment, but I have not time now. . . .
Send as much *prima materia* as you can get gathered in [Scorpio], by
itself; if in [Virgo], by it itselfe.

In addition to his belief in judicial astrology, Allin also followed the
teachings of Culpeper in suggesting that medicinal herbs be gathered
at astrologically propitious times.

In New England, the Reverend Samuel Lee indicated the exact
hour at which a child was born in the records of the Congregational
Church at Bristol, Rhode Island, because, claimed his biographer, he
"had a great reputation as an astrologer," and the hour of birth was
an essential element in casting a horoscope.[32]

Astrological almanacs were first published in New England in 1678,
and by the end of the seventeenth century, the "Man of Signs" came
to be included in many. This diagram demonstrated how the twelve
zodiacal constellations through which the moon and the sun (actually the earth) traveled influenced twelve organs or regions of the body.
The colonial almanac maker and physician, William Ames, explained
the purpose of the anatomy, which he included in his publications
"to please the Country People's eye;/ For if they in this place don't
see his features/ They'll not know at what time to cut their Creatures."
It was considered crucial, in order to treat a particular ailment or to
let blood on a given day, to determine from the almanac whether or
not the moon or sun was in the zodiacal sign which held sway over
the organ or part of the body to be treated. Thomas Palmer urged
that one should "forbear bleeding the member governed of any Sign
the day that the Mem[ber] is in it for fear of the great effusion of
blood that may happen. Nor likewise when the Sun it [*sic*] in it, for
the great danger that may follow thereof."[33]

The Reverend Gershom Bulkeley (HC 1651) of Wethersfield, Connecticut, owned a copy of John Tully's almanac for 1699, whose publications typically contained the "Man of Signs." Astrology also guided
his cures: for the treatment of epilepsy he recommended the "Oile
of mans blood" be taken from "sound young men in spring, a large

quantity," which was then to be purified in "horse dung," a popular component of many colonial remedies. The medicine was to be administered to the epileptic "in peony water every day for an whole month, beginning ye new moon . . . repeated once at every new moone for an whole yeere."[34]

A number of Harvard-educated minister-physicians were almanac makers, yet none of them included the "Man of Signs" in their publications. The theory of the close relationship between the zodiac, moon, and sun and man's body had come under attack in England by the first decade of the seventeenth century. In New England, almanac compilers such as John Tulley of Saybrook, Connecticut, who in response to popular demand included the "Man of Signs," suffered derision at the hands of those who did not. In 1696, the alchemical physician and almanac maker Christian Lodowick of Boston condemned Tulley's "sinfull love of that Soul bewitching Vanity of Star-Prophecy commonly called Astology [*sic*]." Lodowick charged Tulley with seeking to "withdraw Persons from a holy Reliance in God's will & Providence. . . . But is it not Vanity & Impiety, to attempt the Revelation of Secret things that belong unto the Lord our God?" He argued that Tulley's "Conceipts of the Dominion of the Moon in Man's body, as it passeth under the 12 Signs: and . . . the Physical Observations . . . about Letting Blood, Purging & c. when the Moon is in such and such a sign, are things disclaimed by the greatest part of Physicians," and "are but Heathenish Whimzies and Ridiculous Trifles." Both Increase and Cotton Mather were notoriously vocal critics of astrology, and minister-physician almanac makers such as Nathaniel Chauncy (HC 1661), Israel Chauncy (HC 1661), and Samuel Brackenbury (HC 1664) excluded the medical diagram of the "Man of Signs" from their publications, no doubt because they too considered astrological medicine a "Heathenish Whims[y]."[35]

As the writings of Thomas Palmer, Gershom Bulkeley, Ezra Carpenter, John Allin, and others demonstrate, some Puritan ministers who practiced medicine were much more open-minded than others concerning the role of astrology in Galenic medicine. Belief in the palpable influence of the stars on the human body was widespread among the laity in Puritan New England, the castigations of such ministers as Cotton Mather notwithstanding. How such divines as John Allin and Samuel Lee could rationalize the casting of nativities with the dictates of Puritan theology, which held that prognostication through astrology was impious and drew one away from "a holy Reliance in God's will & Providence," is not clear. However, it is obvious that there was no general consensus among New England's preacher-physicians as to the proper boundaries of their medical practice. Also, given the popularity of the "Man of Signs" among the laity, it is highly probable that some patients of these practitioners were reluctant to allow themselves to be bled by the minister unless they felt that the heavens favored such endeavors. The case of the sixteenth-century physician Thomas Erastus illustrates this point. Upon returning to Germany after studying medicine in Italy for nine years, Erastus was greatly displeased when he found that his patients had great faith in almanacs. Because his patients would refuse to be bled on a certain day due to the almanac's astrological admonitions, Erastus grudgingly indulged his patient's fears when he felt there was no danger in doing so.[36] Thus, the demands of the patient population may have influenced a minister's way of providing medical care.

Astrological medicine, such as that promoted by Culpeper, was based on the macrocosm-microcosm analogy, with man in the center of a complex system of correspondences between the celestial and the terrestrial worlds. The knowledge of herbs and their astrological rulership had held a respected place in medical practice for many centuries.[37] Astrological predictions were much in vogue during Cromwell's reign and were spread throughout the English public in the form of printed leaflets. A number of Puritan pamphleteers, such as John Webster, deplored the neglect of astrology in the universities, which many reformers viewed as a utilitarian science. Astrological predictions also became an integral part of millenarian literature after 1640; the prediction of the Apocalypse was used by Puritan reformers to engender support for the Long Parliament, which they characterized as "God's agent of reformation" for ridding the established church and the government of corruption.[38] Thus the use of astrology, even in guiding humoral intervention in medicine, had broad political and religious ramifications, especially for Puritans. And many New England colonists no doubt were aware of the rampant astrological prophesying in the mother country. Yet, if the physician and almanac maker Christian Lodowick was correct, most orthodox physicians rejected the role of astrology in medicine. It is important to keep in mind, however, that orthodox "regular" physicians, such as the kind licensed by the Royal College of Physicians in London, were a rarity in New England until the middle decades of the eighteenth century.

In discussing the influence of occultism in early America, Jon Butler recently argued that, when such elites as Benjamin Franklin in the colonies and Jonathan Swift in England ridiculed occultism and the practice of astrology, the masses tended to defer "to elite opinion" and abandon such beliefs. But in England, astrological almanacs flourished throughout the eighteenth century and even into the nineteenth, much as in America. Many astrological magazines were produced in nineteenth-century England, attesting to the longevity of such occult concepts as astrology. In New England, such members of the educated elite as the minister Ezra Carpenter (HC 1720) continued to record astrological information relevant to the practice of medicine in their private writings well into the eighteenth century. The topic also continued to be a subject of academic debate at Harvard until the Revolutionary era: in 1728, one student for the master's degree responded negatively to the thesis topic, "Do medicinal herbs operate by planetary power?" In 1762, another student defended the concept that the planets and stars influence terrestrial events. Although belief in astrology waned in England and America over the course of the eighteenth century, a segment of the clergy, much like the laity, maintained a belief in natural astrology as it related to medical practices.[39]

Certainly one of the most consistent features of the libraries surveyed from clerical estate inventories, which spanned from 1675 to 1820, is the presence of the pharmacopoeia or dispensatory (which was in English), in 94 percent of the libraries surveyed. (A number of these were written from the iatrochemical perspective, to be addressed in the following chapter.) The erudite Cotton Mather, a fellow of the most prestigious scientific organization of England, the Royal Society, not surprisingly was the only minister whose library lacked one of the popular dispensatories. In the "Angel of Bethesda," completed in 1724, he argued that "our Herbals give such poor, sorry, deficient, false and undistinguishing Accounts, of the Vertues of Simples, that we must not Venture to practice upon their Authority." He felt that "while the *Spagyrical* Gentlemen [i.e., alchemists] sometimes too much *Neglect* the Simple *Vegetable*, the *Galenical* do too much *Confound* it, by mixing a needless Heap of Plants together in their Medicines." Mather was familiar with the astrological-Galenical herbals of Culpeper and Salmon, as well as with some of the "spagyrical" pharmacopoeia of Germanic and Dutch origin. He was, however, exceptional in his criticism of the dispensatories so popular among the bulk of clerics, physicians, and laity alike. And the dispensatory, the preeminently practical medical guide of the era, with its mixture of orthodox humoral and astrological medicine, retained its popularity well past the end of the colonial era. It would appear that some ministers, who were indeed part of the educated elite in their communities, had greater affinity for popular medicine than the more orthodox brand favored by men like Cotton Mather.[40]

In sum, Galenic humoral theory, often intermixed with astrological concepts, was an integral part of medical practice for many cleric-physicians of Puritan New England. Not only did a majority of the ministers collect dispensatories with a humoral orientation, but also their personal remedy collections often display a familiarity with and adherence to some of the basic tenets of Galenic theory. An examination of a number of the sermons and poems of the ministers in this study also reveals that their knowledge of Galenic humoralism deeply affected their religious modes of expression; Galenic metaphors describing the condition of the soul were widely used, particularly during the seventeenth century. A natural result of the dual profession, as well as an artifact of a precedent stretching back to ancient Greece, the language of humoral pathology became the minister's tool for exploring and articulating religious themes.

One of the interesting findings of this examination of personal clerical dispensatories is that a widespread medical information network existed in colonial New England. The minister collected his remedies through local and extralocal connections, from individuals and from medical texts he collected or borrowed. In a sense, ministers, particularly those in rural and frontier settings, such as Edward Taylor and Ebenezer Parkman, acted as "brokers" for information which they disseminated to the community. Puritan divines regularly attended clerical conventions and association meetings and often exchanged pulpits with colleagues; the rural minister, in particular, traveled out of the county more frequently than the majority of his flock, so he was able to stay abreast of political and economic trends in the region. And, by the eighteenth century, newspapers and magazines became an important source of information. Such ministers as Ebenezer Parkman collected them with great tenacity, patiently copying the latest medical remedies from their pages. While clerical authority certainly had declined by the early decades of the eighteenth century, the minister still was an exceptional member of his community in colonial times. His learning and his extensive network of connections beyond and within the parish dictated his role as an intermediary between the parish and the outside world.[41] Not the least important aspects of this role were interpreting and disseminating medical information, providing news of the approach of the dreaded "flux" (dysentery) or the throat distemper into the region, and deciding which remedies would be most appropriate for local disease outbreaks. The well-documented contentiousness of colonial New England churches notwithstanding, the minister often was viewed as trustworthy and as having a discerning eye for truth and fraud. Therefore his *"probatio est"* (highest recommendation, based on repeated trial) of a given remedy typically had credibility within the community, regardless of whether or not it was based on Galenic or Paracelsian theory.

Chapter 4

In Search of the Philosopher's Stone

"There is a thre[e] fold Substance in Vegitables, Minerals & Animals called Sal[t], Sulphur, Mercury," explained the Reverend Thomas Palmer in his *vade mecum* of 1696. The minister of colonial Middleborough, Massachusetts, was familiar with these principles of Paracelsian theory because he had consulted a number of books on chemical medicine during the preparation of his *vade mecum*. He drew upon Johann Schroeder's *Pharmacopoeia medico-chymica* (1641), John French's *The Art of Distillation, or A Treatise of the choicest Spagyricall Preparations* (1651), and John Woodall's *The Surgions Mate* (1617), all of which contained the principles of the Paracelsian chemical doctrine.[1] The medical doctrine known as "iatrochemistry" (which translates as "chemistry applied to medicine" or "the chemistry of doctors") gained wide acceptance among New England's Puritan divines engaged in the healing arts over the course of the seventeenth century. In fact, iatrochemical works were as popular as Nicholas Culpeper's publications in the libraries of New England's cleric-physicians, appearing in 47 percent of the collections surveyed (see table 3.1). What were the factors which contributed to the appeal of iatrochemistry to the minister-physicians of colonial New England? Was their interest in reading and collecting texts on chemical medicine carried over to their medical practice? How did the new chemical doctrine mesh with the pre-existing Galenic medical model? These questions perhaps can best be addressed by first exploring the fundamental elements of the mysterious iatrochemical doctrine, and by tracing the transfer of interest in chemical medicine from Europe to the New England colonies.

The revolutionary chemical medical movement of the sixteenth century was engendered by the alchemical teachings of the Swiss physician, Paracelsus (Theophrastus Bombastus von Hohenheim, 1493–

1541). By the end of the sixteenth century, the alchemical writings of Paracelsus had attracted a large following, which included the monarchs of England and Scotland, theologians of varying degrees of conformity and nonconformity, scholars, aristocrats, gentry, and physicians throughout Europe. Paracelsus's mystical writings defiantly called for a rejection of the conservative scholasticism of Galenic medicine, and a heated debate over the superiority of the two doctrines exploded in England during the middle decades of the seventeeth century—a debate deeply rooted in the social, political, and religious controversies that led to the Puritan Revolution.[2]

Reading Paracelsus, one encounters a bizarre world of mystical principles, macrocosms and microcosms, and a blend of gnostic, hermetic, and biblical elements.[3] Rather than the Galenic system of diagnosis and treatment, which was based on the four bodily humors and the related qualities of hot, dry, moist, and cold, Rev. Palmer understood the *tria prima* (the three principles of salt, sulphur, and mercury) as the essential factors in Paracelsian diagnosis and therapy. Always couched in religious symbolism, this triad was considered "most perfect" because it "agreeth with the everlasting Trinity."[4] The Paracelsians believed that the three principles of salt, sulphur, and mercury were present in all matter. John Woodall, the Paracelsian surgeon whose text (*The Surgions Mate*) was popular in England as well as among some New England divines, explained:

> The *Sal*, *Sulphur*, and *Mercury* are by the Ancients divided out as followeth: they affirme the thin Volatile and watery part or substance of anything whether it be animall or not; to be the Mercuriall part thereof; the fatty oiley, or any way combustible part to be the Sulphurious part of the same medicine, and the ashes remaining after combustion is esteemed the Salt part thereof.

Thus, in Paracelsian phraseology, the term "salt" did not refer to the chemical compound as we know it, but to a principle inherent in matter which remains after combustion. In verse, Woodall described the *tria prima* as "the Mercurie that's volatill,/ the Sulphur burnes like fire:/ The Sal in fundo doth remaine,/ as christals their desire."[5] Diseases were classified into three categories based on the *tria prima*: eruptions of the skin indicated the presence of a saline disease; sulphurous conditions were manifested by inflammations and fevers; mercurial infirmities were characterized by excessive moisture and were treated with specific "chemical species" of mercury, and so on.

Through the alchemical furnace, the "chymist" would separate the "archeus" or spiritual principle of a plant, root, mineral, or animal from its material substratum, which would distinguish the pure from the impure elements. The *archei* were considered to be the mystical and vital forces in nature, the essence of life, present in all matter, all species; in fact, the iatrochemists held that there were as many archei in the world as there were species. Therapy was directed at restoring the harmony of the archei (virtues) in the body with purified medicines created through the chemical art.[6]

The iatrochemists believed that medicines were imprisoned by their intermixture with baser substances, much as man's soul was housed in his corrupt flesh, and only through the "artifical Anatomy of the Chymists" in the furnace could purified medicines be produced. After Adam's transgression, the medicinal properties of minerals, animals, and plants were no longer revealed to man by God directly. Only through arduous labor in the alchemical laboratory could one "release" medicines into a form which would be beneficial to humanity, bringing man closer to a reversal of the effects of the Fall, closer to physical and spiritual perfection, and closer to God.[7] In his *Basilica Chymica* (1609), the Paracelsian popularizer and systematizer Oswald Croll (ca. 1560–1690) explained that "Chymistry . . . doth make manifest, not onely the true Simples, Wonders, Secrets, Mysteries, Vertues, Forces respecting health, but also . . . it teacheth . . . to free medicines from those scurvy raggs wherein they were wrapt up." The Reverend Thomas Palmer characterized the chemical process in his "Limbic" (alembic, a chemical apparatus used to distill medicines) as a "Universal cleanser, a universal healer, a Universal emptier of all impuritys." After separating the impurities out of medicinal preparations, only the pure essence, or "Quintessence," remained. "For my own part," he boasted, "it is the best preparation of medicine that is or can be made." Second only to the healing powers of God himself, Palmer placed great faith in Paracelsian chemical technique, and he

believed that "most of the medicines of other physitians . . . are . . .
Crude, impure and gross, and clogged with terrestrial thicknes."[8]

Since the Middle Ages, theologians like the English Franciscan Roger
Bacon (1214–94) had expressed a strong affinity for the mysterious art
of alchemy. While many would define alchemy as the attempt to
transmute base metals into gold, to its adepts the art was deeply religious in signification, a major factor in its widespread popularity among
Puritan divines. Even Martin Luther warmly embraced the practice
and, like most alchemical authors of the sixteenth and seventeenth
centuries, drew analogies between chemical processes in the alembic
and the spiritual transformation of the heart and soul which accompanied the laboratory procedures:

> The science of alchymy I like very well, and indeed 'tis the philos-
> ophy of the ancients. I like it not only for the profits it brings in melt-
> ing metals, in decocting, preparing, extracting, and distilling herbs,
> roots: I like it also for the sake of allegory and secret significance, which
> is exceedingly fine, touching the resurrection of the dead at the last day.
> For, as in a furnace the fire extracts and separates from substance other
> portions, and carries upward the spirit, the life, the sap, the strength,
> while the unclean matter, the dregs, remain at the bottom, like a dead,
> worthless carcass; even so God at the day of judgment, will separate
> all things through fire, the righteous from the ungodly. The Christians
> and righteous shall ascend upwards into heaven, and there live everlast-
> ingly, but the wicked and ungodly, as the dross and filth, shall remain
> in hell, and there be damned.[9]

The desired goal was purification and perfection: the creation of the
Philosopher's Stone or, through the grace of God, the moral and
spiritual regeneration of the believer's soul, thus paving the way for
salvation on Judgment Day.[10]

By the mid-seventeenth century, Oswald Croll's *Basilica Chymica*
had become one of the standard texts on iatrochemistry in Europe
as well as among Puritan preacher-physicians in New England. His
Latin treatise was present in 21 percent of the libraries surveyed, and
those who owned it were practicing medicine throughout the second
half of the seventeenth century and the early decades of the eighteenth.
No doubt the strong Calvinist tone of this work greatly appealed

to New England clerics. Unlike the Catholic Paracelsus, Croll portrays a stern and forbidding God, the "Greatest and Eternall Judge (whose Terrible and Ineffable Majesty all mortall men ought to stand in fear of) who at the Judgement day will examine our deserts." Croll provides his readers with a unique synthesis of hermeticism and Calvinism; he emphasizes the doctrine of justification by faith alone and the futility of man's works in attaining salvation, the doctrine of the elect and the notion of idleness as sin. The *Basilica Chymica* was a politically motivated work, dedicated to Croll's patron, the Calvinist Prince Christian of Anhalt, who attempted to forge an Evangelical Union of Protestant Princes to stave off the advances of the House of Hapsburg.[11]

The writings of the Flemish physician and disciple of Paracelsus, Johannes Baptista van Helmont (1579–1644), were even more popular among the ministers in this study than those of Croll, appearing in roughly one third of the collections examined. The Reverend Phineas Fiske, a graduate of Yale's class of 1704, acquired his volume early in the eighteenth century, and even the newly established library at Yale possessed a copy of Helmont's works, as well as the text by Croll. Van Helmont's bitter struggles against the Catholic Church in his native Spanish-controlled Brussels were well known in Protestant circles. The Louvain Theological Faculty had castigated van Helmont for his acceptance of the "monstrous superstitions" of the Paracelsian school, and "for having spread more than Cimmerian darkness all over the world by his chemical philosophy (*pyrotechnice philosophando*)." No doubt his aversion to Catholicism and his association with the Calvinist and Lutheran doctrines contributed to the popularity of his publications among English protestants.[12]

Although, in the *Institutes*, Calvin vehemently denounced all forms of natural magic,[13] many adepts saw clear-cut parallels between the Calvinist doctrine which informed their Puritan theology and the mysteries of alchemy. The case of the Puritan minister and alchemist of Elizabethan England, William Blomfild (died ca. 1575), provides evidence that even orthodox Calvinists were receptive to alchemy well before the art was associated with the radical Puritan sects forged during the turbulent Revolutionary decades. In one of Blomfild's poems, entitled the "Regiment of Lyfe," he states that he is convinced that the knowledge of the alchemist is a divine gift: "From God it cometh, and God maketh it sensible/ To some Elect, to others he doth it denay." Here Blomfild interprets the Calvinist doctrine of the elect as signifying the alchemical "adept"; just as God freely bestows his grace on those elected for salvation, so he grants spiritual perfection to his chosen "adepts," making them worthy of attaining the Philosopher's Stone. Again, in Calvinist phraseology, Blomfild explains, "This Parallisme [*sic*] shewes/ That the Regeneration of Man and the Purification of Mettall haue like degrees of Preparation and Operation to their highest perfection."[14]

New England divines also employed alchemical allusion and metaphor in their poetry, sermons, and other writings to convey Christian meaning and to heighten religious themes. In fact, those minister-physicians known to have a familiarity with the new chemical doctrine often displayed this knowledge in both their medical and their religious writings. Alchemical imagery previously had been used for satirical purposes (as well as to embellish the beauty of nature) in English popular literature from the Middle Ages through the seventeenth century. Chaucer satirized the alchemist in *The Canon Yeoman's Tale*, as did Ben Jonson after him in *The Alchemist*. Yet during the late sixteenth and early seventeenth centuries, as the iatrochemical movement gained momentum in many parts of Europe, alchemy's literary functions began to undergo a subtle transformation. With the publication of the deeply religious writings of Paracelsus, Jacob Boehme, and the "English Paracelsians," alchemical imagery, particularly in the poetry of English Protestants, became infused with religious signification and was used as a vehicle to describe the inner process of purification, the spiritual and moral transformation of the Christian soul. Alchemy melded with the eschatological and millenarian themes of Calvinist theology, as the poem by Blomfild discussed above demonstrates.[15]

Influenced by the poetry and iatrochemical publications of the mother country, New England divines also employed alchemical imagery when describing the doctrine of salvation. For example, the voice of Michael Wigglesworth's (HC 1651) "Distressed Conscience" expressed a fear that he would depart this world "nothing else but dross/ And sinner reprobate,/ That is not purify'd/ By passing through the fire." Wigglesworth's impressive medical library housed a number of iatrochemical works, such as the popular *Basilica Chymica* of Oswald Croll, indicating his familiarity with alchemical themes.[16]

For the New England Puritan, poetry was a vehicle for soul-searching and for setting forth "the Glory of God." The Reverend Edward Taylor frequently employed alchemical metaphor in his writings for this purpose:

> God Chymist is, doth Sharon's Rose distill.
>   Oh! Choice Rose Water! Swim my Soul
>   herein.
> Let Conscience bibble in it with her Bill.
>   Its Cordiall, ease doth Heart burns Causd
>   by Sin.
> Oyle, Syrup, Sugar, and Rose Water such.
>   Lord, give, give, give; I cannot have
>   too much.[17]

The chemist distilling medicinal preparations represents God who, when willing, can heal the sin-sick soul. In another poem Taylor becomes the "Violl" (vial), the receptacle for the "heavenly Choice drugs" created in God's "Humane Frame" which takes the form of "A Golden Still." For Taylor, both the chemical practitioner and the alembic itself represent God, the great transformer of man's soul; and the medicines chemically prepared in the alembic symbolize God's saving grace.[18]

One of the most popular poets of the English metaphysical school (even among orthodox Puritans), was the Anglican cleric, George Herbert. In *The Countrey Parson*, Herbert maintained that "the Country Parson desires to be all to his Parish, and not only a Pastour, but . . . a Phisician." Although Herbert recommends that the Galenic texts of Fernelius and an herbal be the parson's medical guidebooks, his poetry also contains alchemical metaphors. In "The Elixir" (the Philosopher's Stone of the alchemists, which allegedly turned metals into gold), he suggests that man should partake of the "tincture," or Christ, in order to "grow bright and clean," to attain a moral and spiritual transformation: "This is the famous Stone/ That turneth all to gold:/

For that which God doth/ touch [i.e., test] and own/ Cannot for lesse be told." Here Christ is the Philosopher's Stone, the catalyst, able to transform the "unclean" sinner into a state of purity (gold).[19] Taylor almost certainly read Herbert's poetry as a schoolboy in Leicestershire, and his writing similarly employs the alchemical metaphor:

> Gold in its Ore, must melted be, to bring
> It midwift from its mother womb: requires
> To make it shine and a rich market thing,
> A fining Pot, and Test, and melting fire.
> So do I, Lord, before thy grace do shine
> In mee, require, thy fire may mee refine.[20]

Taylor employs the metaphor of gold melted in the alchemical furnace, much as Herbert did, to symbolize the purification of his sinful soul. Taylor, like so many other Puritans, believed that regeneration had to be preceded by destruction or dissolution, in this case symbolized by the refining process of the "melting fire."

It has been suggested recently that Taylor's poetry reflects a complete rejection of the practical aspects of the alchemical art, and that alchemy was not taken seriously by Taylor and other "rational" thinkers by the end of the seventeenth century. In one poem Taylor had written:

> The Boasting Spagyrist (Insipid Phlegm,
> Whose words outstrut the Sky) vaunts
> he hath rife
> The Water, Tincture, Lozenge, Gold, and Gem,
> Of Life itselfe. But here's the
> Bread of Life.
> I'le lay my life, his Aurum Vitae Red
> Is to my Bread of Life, worse than
> DEAD HEAD.[21]

Taylor completed this poem in 1684, when, in both old and New England, iatrochemistry was still flourishing. Of course, the doctrine had its critics. One author, ridiculing *Mr Culpeper's Treatise of Aurum Potabile*, described these practitioners as follows:

> Chymists, of whom a man may say as St Paul spake of the Cretians,
> that they are evil beasts, always liars, regarding nothing but their bel-
> lies; thay are great boasters, but small performers, and like Taylors emi-
> nent for nothing but their long bills, who if they come once to be
> known, vanish into ayre like the smoak of their own furnaces.[22]

In a less caustic tone, Sir Thomas Browne complained, "I wish . . .
the chymists had been more sparing; who, over-magnifying their preparations, inveigle the curiosity of many, and delude the security of
most." The mystical search for the Philosopher's Stone obviously led
some chemists to make excessive claims and indulge in flights of fancy.[23]

John Allin, who had graduated from Harvard College in 1643 and
then removed to England to practice both divinity and physic, criticized his fellow "chymicall practitioners," who "were too confident
[tha]t their chemical medicines" could cure the plague:

> They would give money for the most infected body they could heare
> of to dissect, which [th]ey had, and opened to search the seate of this
> disease, & c., upon [th]e opening wherof a stinch ascended from the
> body, and infected them every one, and it is said they are all dead
> since. . . . God is resolved to staine the pride of all glory; there is no
> boasting before Him, and much lesse ag[ain]st Him.

Many an English hermeticist, overly confident of his ability to bring
about miraculous cures, exaggerated claims of producing the Philosopher's Stone or the Universal Elixir (panacea). Edward Taylor criticized the overweening pride of many chemical authorities and physicians, which he, like Allin, considered an affront to God. Although he
was critical of the sinful pride of some of the chemical physicians of
his acquaintance, Allin nevertheless was a disciple of Paracelsus. His
correspondence is filled with references to alchemically prepared medicines, such as the plague remedy known as "materia prima." Paracelsus
had taught that this plant ("nostock" or "cerefolium") fell from the
heavens during the night. Allin had set up "divers chemical stills and
one furnace" for the preparation of remedies such as this. During the
plague epidemic of 1665, he recommended to a friend that he "get
a piece of angell gold, if you can . . . w[hi]ch is phylospohicall gold,

and keepe it allways in yo[u]r mouth when you walke out or any sicke persons come to you: you will find strange effects of it for good in freedome of breathing, & c. as I have done."[24] Although Allin was a chemical practitioner himself, perhaps his training in divinity caused him to set some limitations on the degree of faith he placed in the efficacy of his medicinal preparations. As Michael Wigglesworth explained, man must beware of "too much going out of the heart in hopes of curing the distemper of the body by the use of some contrived means"; it was a sin when the Puritan placed more hope in the efficacy of natural remedies than in the will of God. Man was justified in using chemical medicines or other natural means to attempt to cure illness, but the Puritans felt that one should humbly acknowledge that the success of such efforts was determined not "infallibly by the greatest Sufficiency of Men, or Second Causes," but by God.[25]

An examination of Taylor's manuscript "Dispensatory" not only reveals his familiarity with Galenic humoralism, but also it contains a lengthy section on chemical theory and remedies. Taylor copied passages from the alchemical treatise by the Puritan minister John Webster, *Metallographia: Or, an History of Metals* (1671), and owned John Woodall's Paracelsian surgical treatise, *The Surgions Mate* (1617), and Johann Schroeder's *Pharmacopoeia Medico-Chymica* (1644). Thus Taylor was familiar with the writings of some prominent iatrochemical authors and was impressed enough with the practical aspects of the doctrine to fill seventy-five pages of his "Dispensatory" with directions for the preparation and administration of chemical medicaments.[26] Taylor, like other ministers and lay health practitioners in colonial New England who employed chemical preparations in their practices, may not have been a disciple of the mystical schools of Paracelsus and van Helmont; but he was, as his poetry, medical manuscripts, and library contents reveal, quite familiar with chemical processes and medications. And his familiarity with iatrochemical texts, evident in his medical writings, obviously carried over into the medical care he provided to his parishioners.

It is, of course, difficult to demonstrate a direct connection between the use of alchemical metaphor in a minister's writings and the presence of iatrochemical texts in his library. But it is probable that such texts exerted an influence on a clergyman's thought patterns, leading him to draw analogies in his writings between, on the one hand, such Puritan themes as the doctrine of the elect, the Last Judgment, and salvation, and, on the other hand, the transformation of base substances into medicinal agents in the chemical furnace. As indicated above, such analogies were pervasive in the iatrochemical texts which New England divines collected and used in their medical practices, as well as in the poetry of such popular poets as George Herbert. The common use of alchemical metaphor to portray religious themes in the English poetry and sermons of the period, and the strongly Protestant tone of iatrochemical texts, seem to have been important factors in the warm reception given to the new chemical medicine in Puritan New England.

While the majority of New England's early iatrochemists were graduates of Harvard College who became cleric-physicians, the graduate who achieved the most recognition as an adept, George Starkey (or Stirk), only pursued the path of the physician. He had entered Harvard College in 1643 and claimed that he "first began the Study of *Chymical Philosophy*" in 1644, during his sophomore year. He also received "good Incouragement" from the famous alchemical physician, John Winthrop, Jr., governor of the Connecticut Colony. At Harvard, Starkey rejected the Peripatetic philosophy which dominated the curriculum, and, after reading Galen, Sennert, and Fernel in his free time, turned to the iatrochemists in the hope of finding "a secure way of curing Diseases." He was successfully practicing medicine in the Boston-Cambridge area in 1647, after receiving his bachelor's degree but before receiving the master's degree (as was not uncommon during the colonial period). Between 1645 and 1647, he befriended the alchemist Robert Child, the noted critic of the New England Way. He removed to England in 1650, where he met a group of chemical practitioners and soon became one of the most prominent iatrochemical authors of his time. He is best known as the formulator of "Starkey's Pill," a fairly weak opiate preparation.[27] The case of George Starkey demonstrates that it was indeed possible for a Harvard student to pursue extracurricular alchemical studies.

While there was no formal instruction in medicine or chemistry at

Harvard during the seventeenth century, at least two of its earliest presidents had envisioned otherwise. Leonard Hoar (HC 1650), a minister-physician, had demonstrated his commitment to establishing a chemical laboratory and chemical instruction at the college soon after he returned from medical studies at Cambridge University and became president of Harvard. While in England, he had come under the influence of the Puritan scientist Robert Boyle, whose works blending the theories of iatrochemistry and iatromechanism soon were added to the college library. In a 1672 letter to his friend Boyle (the same year he began his term as Harvard's president), Hoar described the changes he envisioned for the young school, including "a laboratory chemical for those philosophers, that by their senses would culture their understandings, are in our design, for the students to spend their time of recreation in them; for readings or notions are but husky provender." This letter, in which Hoar is seeking advice from Boyle on how they "may become not only nominal, but real scholars," is provocative, not only in light of the iatrochemical works he collected for his private library and his probable exposure to the chemical doctrine while studying medicine in England, but also because it implies that there were chemical "philosophers" already under his tutelage, and that their "readings or notions" alone were incomplete without the practical instruction which could be gained in the laboratory. The practical or experimental side of the new chemistry appealed deeply to many scientists who adhered to the basic tenets of Baconian experimental philosophy. Hoar's vision never became a reality, and he was forced to resign after only three years in office.[28]

Another Harvard president, the medical practitioner and minister Charles Chauncy, trained his sons in both divinity and physick, and also tutored the prominent cleric-physician Thomas Thacher in these arts. The 1703 estate inventory of Chauncy's son Israel (HC 1661) includes not only works on alchemical medicine, but also such items as "an alimbeck" and "3 Alchimy spoons," indicating Israel's involvement in the art. The correspondence between his brother Isaac (HC 1651) (who had removed to London, where he became a full licentiate of the Royal College of Physicians) and the Reverend Gershom

Bulkeley (HC 1655) of Wethersfield, Connecticut, indicates that Isaac was sending his brother-in-law alchemical glassware from England. "Doctor Isaac Chauncy" also sent Bulkeley a number of his personal chemical remedies at the end of the seventeenth century, providing evidence that the former was involved in the art of chemical medicine.[29]

The commonplace notebook of a third brother, Elnathan Chauncy (HC 1661), presents further evidence of the interest in alchemy among Harvard-educated clergymen. He copied numerous passages from the works of van Helmont, Cornelius Agrippa, and Eiraneous Philalethes (the latter may have been George Starkey's pseudonym). The passages taken from Philalethes make a mockery of Artistotelian science, an essential part of the Harvard curriculum. "We are still hammering the old elements," he wrote, "but seeke not the America that lys beyond them."[30] From a study of Harvard College Commencement *Theses* and *Questiones* from the seventeenth century, a more widespread interest in chemical medicine in its philosophical form can be discerned. For example, at commencement in 1687, Nehemiah Walter received his Master of Arts degree for defending the topic, *An detur lapis aurificus?* (Is a gold-producing stone possible?). On this evidence, I. Bernard Cohen concludes, "Defenders of alchemy were plainly not lacking at seventeenth-century Harvard."[31]

In 1687, two years after the Puritan divine Charles Morton had migrated to New England, anticipating (but not receiving) an appointment as Harvard's next president, his scientific manuscript known as the "Compendium Physicae" was introduced at the college as a physics text—a status it retained for the next forty years. His "Compendium" included an unusual blend of the physical theories of Aristotle, Descartes, and Boyle, as well as several lengthy passages on practical chemistry and alchemy ("Artifice of Gold by Alchymy" and "The Finding of the Philosopher's Stone"), arts which he considered highly credible. It has been suggested that Morton's text may have been instrumental in stimulating an interest in alchemy and practical chemistry among some Harvard students of the late seventeenth and early eighteenth centuries. Cohen argues that interest in chemistry declined at Harvard between 1717 and 1779, and that Newtonian mechanics and astronomy were stressed in its place. It was not until after the American Revolution that chemistry, in its practical form, again was actively pursued at Harvard.[32]

As in England, a network of chemical practitioners who corresponded and exchanged medical information had developed in New England after the mid-seventeenth century, which included the ministers Gershom Bulkeley and Samuel Lee, and the physicians John Winthrop, Jr.; Christian Lodowick of Bristol, Rhode Island (who had recently converted from Quakerism to Congregationalism); and James Oliver of Cambridge, Massachusetts. All of these men had highly successful medical practices. Their hermetic experimentation was fused with "formidable doses of mystical theology and transcendental philosophy, in the true Paracelsian manner." Both Lee and Lodowick had migrated to New England late in the seventeenth century; no doubt their reputations as chemical healers stimulated interest in the iatrochemical doctrine among some colonials and provided models for them to emulate. According to Thomas Prince, Dr. James Oliver had engaged in the "Art of *Chymistry* [with] . . . the ingenious *Dr. Lodowick a German*, who was also accounted an excellent *Physician*, and the most skilful *Chymist* that ever came to these Parts of *America*."[33] And Cotton Mather praised Samuel Lee's skills, claiming that "hardly ever a more universally learned person trod the American strand."[34] Although Lee, who possessed a fine library of over 1,200 volumes, many of them alchemical and occult, was critical of the lack of professional structure and skill among many health practitioners in New England, he praised "one Dr. Avery . . . [who] was a great inquirer and had skill in Helmont & chemicall physick." The Reverend Michael Wigglesworth sought Avery's medical services when he thought he was suffering from gonorrhea.[35]

In a letter to the Reverend Bulkeley, Dr. Oliver criticized an alchemical text from which Bulkeley had copied lengthy passages (*Four Bookes of Johannes Segerus Weidenfeld, Concerning the Secrets of the Adepts*, London, 1685). According to Oliver, "Many notable things he [Weidenfeld] did, & many more he might have done in the practice of Physicke, had he not been too enthusiasticall in his Divinity & Philosophy."[36] Thus, there was perhaps a sense among some adepts that "Divinity" interfered with the advancement of the art. It is interesting to note that both Gershom Bulkeley and Thomas Palmer, who were known to have practiced the chemical arts, abandoned the ministry fairly early in their careers and carried on a flourishing medical practice. Perhaps, as Oliver suggested, their divinity "got in the way" of their alchemical investigations.

The widespread fame and popularity of the chemical techniques of John Winthrop, Jr., whom Cotton Mather named "Hermes Christianus," as well as the successful practices of those Harvard-educated ministers and the physicians discussed above, demonstrate that chemical medicine enjoyed a high degree of popularity in New England throughout the seventeenth century. This finding is hardly surprising, given that the same situation prevailed among Puritans in England as well. By the 1640s and 1650s, partisans of English iatrochemistry had forged a cohesive social movement, bolstered by the vast numbers of Paracelsian publications published in the vernacular. Although not all Paracelsian and hermetic writings came from Puritan sources, many English translators of Paracelsus and iatrochemical authors held strong Parliamentarian and Puritan sentiments. And the iatrochemical movement itself was closely affiliated with the political and religious tendencies of the Puritan reformers. No doubt this factor contributed to the popularity of chemical medicine among New England divines and lay practitioners alike.[37]

John Winthrop, Jr., corresponded closely with Samuel Hartlib and other Puritan leaders of the iatrochemical movement in England and then communicated his knowledge to other colonials involved in the movement. These English spokesmen vociferously attacked the Royal College of Physicians for its attempts to monopolize health care in England and its attachment to scholasticism and the "heathen" Galen. Swept up by the antimonopolistic mood of a Puritan-controlled Parliament, "chymicall" physicians led an all-out pamphlet war against the college; they also encroached upon the college's domain by providing health care to those members of the populace unwilling and/or unable to resort to the costly "regular" physicians. The college claimed the legal right to control and license medical practitioners within a seven-mile radius of London, and membership in this body was strictly limited to a privileged group of medical graduates of the universities. The college felt threatened by the competing group of iatrochemists, yet, as long as Parliament was under Puritan control, it could not prosecute illegal practitioners. Thus, a grassroots health-care coalition, championed by the iatrochemists, decidedly antimonopolistic, rapidly gained adherents throughout England. This movement proved impossible for the Royal College to control, and its antimonopolistic battle cry found a sympathetic ear across the ocean among a select group of New England colonists.[38]

In New England, no monopolistic group of physicians like the Royal College developed during the colonial period. The so-called "regular" or "orthodox" physicians, such as those who graduated with degrees in medicine from Cambridge, Oxford, or continental universities and became licentiates of the Royal College of Physicians of London, did not immigrate to New England in any numbers before 1720. Dr. William Douglass (c. 1691–1752), the acerbic critic of Cotton Mather's "meddling" in medical matters during the inoculation controversy of 1721, after studying medicine in Edinburgh, Leiden, and Utrecht (M.D., 1712), immigrated to Boston and set up shop as the only professionally-trained doctor in town. One of the few university-educated physicians to come to New England before Douglass was Dr. Robert Child. He had come to Boston in 1644, after receiving his Doctor of Medicine degree from Padua in 1638. An iatrochemist, he was imprisoned for sedition and forced to return to England in 1647. Although the alchemical "Dr." Lodowick took his master's degree in Leipzig (c. 1680), he probably never took the degree of Doctor of Medicine. Thus, the most famous practitioners of seventeenth-century New England, such as Lodowick and John Winthrop, Jr., were not professionally trained and were iatrochemists. Therefore the "elite" physician who served as a model for other healers—including clerics—to emulate was the chemical practitioner. The ministers Gershom Bulkeley and Samuel Lee surely fit into this category of practitioner, probably influenced by Winthrop, from whom at least one of them (Bulkeley) learned chemical remedies. Chemical practitioners like Bulkeley and Lee exemplify the mainstream of what was considered "professional" and "orthodox" medicine in seventeenth-century

New England.[39] In part, this predominance of chemical practitioners may be explained by the dearth of university-trained physicians in New England. But it may have resulted in part from the antimonopolistic sentiments of New England Puritans. Given the antagonism towards the Anglican-dominated Royal College of Physicians articulated by many of their Puritan brethren in England, it is hardly surprising that an organization to control medical licensure was not developed in the United States until the formation of the American Medical Association nearly two centuries later, in the nineteenth century.

There has been a strong tendency for a number of historians of Puritan England, such as Christopher Hill, Keith Thomas, Charles Webster, and others, to associate the radical Puritan sects which flowered during the interregnum with the iatrochemical movement which grew in momentum during the same period. They have suggested that the splintering of English Puritanism during the middle decades of the seventeenth century led to a sympathetic reception of Neoplatonism, alchemy, and natural magic among the more radical sects. The combining of alchemy with eschatology and millenarianism is especially prevalent in the publications of the radical Puritan sects, groups which the Presbyterian Thomas Hall described as being of the "Familistical-Levelling-Magical Temper."[40]

P.M. Rattansi and Charles Webster argue that the Puritan Revolution created an ideal intellectual climate for the development of Paracelsian iatrochemistry. Paracelsian medicine, from its Reformation origins, was closely associated with Protestant mysticism. The mystical, antirational aspects of the teachings of Paracelsus were deeply appealing in times of crisis, when people naturally sought "in supernatural 'illumination' an ideological sanction for acts which overthrew the established order in state and church"; therefore, "that side of the Paracelsian and Helmontian doctrine which exalted the knowledge of illumination above that derived from 'carnal reason' had a particular attraction for reformers and revolutionaries," Rattansi states. These Christian mystics, much like many anti-Galenist medical writers of the period, denounced the scholasticism of the Christian dogmatists. As a reaction against the rigidity of established religion, many Puritans sought out and probed alternative readings for religious inspiration, such as the Jewish Cabala, the hermeticists, alchemical texts, and Neoplatonic natural magic treatises.[41]

A study of the library holdings of New England's medical ministry reveals that, in addition to iatrochemical texts, the clerics also sought out and collected works on hermeticism and the occult sciences, works which were both mystical and deeply religious in nature. Similarly, in England, iatrochemists (often radical Puritans) also delved into such mystical writings. After Harvard's president, the minister-physician Leonard Hoar, died in 1675, his widow allowed Increase Mather to come and select some books from his library, since Mather had lost much of his own collection in a fire. Mather chose two treatises on natural magic, *De occulta philosophia* (1533) by Henry Cornelius Agrippa and Giovanni Baptista Della Porta's *Magiae naturalis* (1558); two works on Rosicrucianism; and van Helmont's famous iatrochemical treatise, *Ortus Medicinae*, among others. Approximately half of the clerical collections surveyed contained such occult, magical works as these, the most popular being works attributed to the supposed founder of the art of alchemy, the mythical Egyptian Hermes Trismegistus, as well as the works of Della Porta and Agrippa. Those ministers who owned iatrochemical works and were known to dabble in alchemy typically collected books on the occult sciences as well, just as many of the "chymicall" physicians and Paracelsian translators and authors of seventeenth-century England explored the mysteries of hermeticism, Cabala magic, and the natural magic tradition of the Florentine school. Students of the young Harvard College had access to treatises on occultism, since the college library contained an extensive collection of such works, including the famous treatise on Christian Cabalist magic, Johannes Reuchlin's *De arte cabalistica* (1587), the works of Pico della Mirandola, treatises on hermeticism, and many others similar in nature (see table 3.1). It would appear that, much as in England, those practitioners (who in this case were also clerics) who were familiar with the tenets of Paracelsianism also took an interest in the obscure philosophies of hermeticism and natural magic. All of these mystical doctrines were interconnected by a Neoplatonic influence which promoted the belief that all matter was imbued with "spirit" and which explained chemical and biological processes within a vitalistic framework.[42]

Frances Yates has characterized the fascination many English Puritans had with the occult sciences (including alchemy) as "Puritan occultism," the origins of which were rooted in the Protestant areas of Europe and which subsequently spread to England—the refuge from anti-Christ—and then to the colonies of New England.[43] Of course, treatises on natural magic and alchemy were by no means "demonic" or affiliated with the black arts. As Della Porta explained in his *Magiae naturalis*, the "works of Magick are nothing else but the works of Nature" which operated through occult (as opposed to manifest) properties and qualities. Critical to the success of magical machinations was the preparation of the operator's mind through a series of "purifying" rituals such as fasting, repentance, and meditation, not unlike those measures used by Purtians in cleansing the soul.[44]

Although the New England preacher-physician's interest in hermeticism and natural magic may have been free of satanic associations, many believed that "Bad Angels have taught People to Cure many Diseases" and that "Good Angels" also could aid healers in curing disease. The Anglican cleric-physician Richard Napier (who, as discussed previously, had a flourishing medical practice outside London from 1597–1634) was known as a Cabalist conjurer who personally communicated with the Archangel Raphael to effect his famous cures. Even Cotton Mather knew of the summoning powers of "Dr. Napier," whom he described as an "old Gentleman of uncommon Devotion and Innocence." Given the atmosphere prevailing in England at the end of the sixteenth and during the seventeenth centuries, in which religion, magic, astrology, alchemy, science, and medicine overlapped, it is hardly surprising that a number of British preacher-physicians, Anglican and Puritan alike, became adherents of these practices, just as their Catholic predecessors had.[45]

Although Perry Miller portrays the terrain of the "New England Mind" as exceptionally rational, given the New England Puritans' fascination with witchcraft and all things supernatural, it is hardly surprising that a number of ministers collected Neoplatonic works on the occult philosophy. These works may have informed their owners' understanding of the preternatural occurrences, events which they dutifully recorded in their diaries and letters. It is conceivable that some of the ministers who were involved in the alchemical arts, such as Samuel Lee, Thomas Palmer, and others, perhaps secretly adhered to a more mystical brand of Protestantism than their orthodox brethren, more akin to the radical Puritan sects of the mother country. Further research on this possibility would bolster recent scholarship on seventeenth-century New England which has demonstrated the presence of more radical strains of thought among some New England Puritans.[46]

In addition to religious and political factors which led to the popularity of chemical medicine in New England, economic factors also played a part in the minister's ability to collect iatrochemical texts and laboratory equipment. Like the practitioner of natural magic, the alchemist "must also be rich," Della Porta explained, "for if we lack money, we shall hardly work in these cases."[47] While it is difficult to characterize the majority of New England divines as "rich," their standard of living typically was better than that of the majority of inhabitants of their communities, allowing them a certain degree of financial flexibility (see chapter 2). The New England divine Thomas Palmer by no means died a poor man. Dissension within Palmer's Middleborough congregation led to his dismissal, yet he continued to practice medicine and perform his "chymicall" distillations in the same community. He raised a large family, put two sons through Harvard, and died in 1743 leaving a healthy estate of over seven thousand pounds.[48] In Connecticut, the Reverend Gershom Bulkeley's medical and surgical practice also was quite extensive and successful, as his surviving medical account books attest. He too resigned from the ministry, "by reason of the weakness of his voice," so the story goes. Bulkeley also practiced law and was a justice of the peace and a political pamphleteer on the side of the Royalists. The precise amount of his estate at death is unknown, but he left a substantial library—nearly 250 volumes, predominantly alchemical—and a large alchemical laboratory to his sons and grandson, and a "negro maid" to his daughter Dorothy. It is interesting to note, as an indication of the value of his alchemical library and laboratory, that after Bulkeley's death, his son John contested that part of his will which bequeathed these items to his favorite grandson Richard Treat.[49]

Clerical as well as lay interest in the chemical arts gradually diminished over the course of the eighteenth century in colonial New England. In 1715, the Reverend John Bulkeley (HC 1699) (son of Gershom Bulkeley), of Colchester, Connecticut, wrote to John Winthrop (III), "I comfort myself . . . that your great retirement is not for naught, and that it will produce some noble discoveries in the Arcana of the chymists, which I promise myself your candour will oblige you to communicate when I shall be so happy as to see you again."[50] But after 1735, only a few of the ministers' estate inventories surveyed contained references to alchemical books or any other occult texts. The Reverend Phineas Fiske (YC 1704; 1681–1738) owned copies of alchemical works by Basil Valentine, Albertus Magnus, Johannes Schroeder, and Sir Kenelm Digby. In fact, one-quarter of Fiske's medical collection was alchemical in nature, a strong indication of his interest in the art. One of Fiske's theological-medical apprentices, the Reverend Moses Bartlett (YC 1730; 1707–1767) also owned Basil Valentine's *The Triumphal Chariot of Antimony* (1660).[51] By the mid-eighteenth century, however, interest in the art of alchemy seems to have waned among the New England intelligentsia, except for a few isolated cases. In the Reverend Ezra Stiles's letter of 1777, in which he emphatically denies accusations made by some of his contemporaries that he was an alchemist, he notes that Benjamin Franklin "told me there were several [alchemists] in Philad[elphi]a & c. who were loosing their Time in chemical Experiments to no Effect."[52] This comment indicates that, while the art still held a fascination for some, many considered such efforts futile. Only one of the thirteen eighteenth-century New England physicians' libraries surveyed contained alchemical or occult works.

A recent study by Allen Debus of the Paracelsian movement in eighteenth-century France points to the persistence of interest in alchemy during the "Age of Reason" in Europe. European interest in alchemy was not simply eclipsed by the iatromathematical school which grew in popularity after Newton's discoveries; rather, there was a gradual movement away from the mystical or spiritual elements of chemistry and toward the more practical, applied aspects of the science.[53]

During the decades preceding the American Revolution, the works of the Leiden professor Herman Boerhaave began to displace the mystical iatrochemical and other occult volumes on the shelves of New England divines. The works of Boerhaave appeared in a third of eighteenth-century minister-physicians' libraries and in 40 percent of contemporary physicians' collections, indicating his widespread appeal among both groups. Boerhaave was the single most influential spokesman for chemical instruction during the early eighteenth century, a time when a search for an organizing explanatory theory for the discipline gained priority over earlier metaphysical approaches. Chemistry took on the guise of a distinct branch of scientific inquiry; as Boerhaave explained,

> Chemistry is an art which teaches the manner of performing certain physical operations, whereby bodies cognizable to the senses, or capable of being rendered cognizable, and of being contained in vessels, are so changed by means of proper instruments, as to produce certain determined effects, and at the same time discover the causes thereof.[54]

As chemistry developed into a more "rational" discipline, separate from the mystical, religious doctrines of the earlier chemical reformers, and separate from the political and social aims of the Puritan iatrochemists of England, the school of iatrochemistry began to lose its appeal for the majority of the minister-physicians of New England.

During the seventeenth century, then, widespread interest in iatrochemistry and the occult sciences among New England divines who engaged in the healing arts was in part stimulated by a pervasive "Puritan occultism" in England. Ministers such as the Reverend John Davenport made frequent trips to England and there procured the most current alchemical books and manuscripts.[55] Popular New England chemical practitioners such as the Reverend Gershom Bulkeley and John Winthrop, Jr., regularly corresponded with Puritan iatrochemists in the mother country, who kept the Americans abreast of current developments in those arts. It cannot be overemphasized, however, that such doctrines as chemical medicine and the natural magic tradition were understood by many intellectuals of this period as distinct, legitimate systems of scientific inquiry into the workings of the natural world and as avenues for exploring the mysterious workings of God's hand in nature. Even the orthodox Cotton Mather owned an extensive collection of occult treatises and had nothing but praise for the skills of such iatrochemists as the Reverend Samuel Lee and John Winthrop, Jr.[56] Cromwell Mortimer, secretary of the prestigious Royal Society of London, of which Winthrop had been elected a member, dedicated a volume of the *Philosophical Transactions* (XL, 1741) to Winthrop, claiming that his "extraordinary knowledge in the deep Mysteries of the most secret Hermetic science" made him "esteemed and courted by learned and good men."[57]

Thus, the atmosphere in early New England, including Harvard College, was congenial to the acceptance of iatrochemistry, particularly among the clergy, because of the confluence of several factors. First and perhaps most important, the art of alchemy was at this time viewed by its adepts as deeply religious in signification, a view reflected in the use of alchemical metaphor in the writings of the clergy, to underscore religious themes. Of the many iatrochemical texts which flooded the market during the seventeenth century, those with a strong Calvinist tone, such as Oswald Croll's *Basilica Chymica*, were deeply appealing to the mentality of many Puritan divines. The warm reception given iatrochemistry by New England minister-physicians paralleled the rise of the doctrine among (often radical) Puritans in England. Like the Puritan leaders of the medical reform movement in the mother country, New England colonists typically were anti-monopolistic and so tended to be sympathetic to the reforming tendencies of the English iatrochemists.

In addition, few regular physicians affiliated with the Royal College of Physicians of London immigrated to the New England colonies. Only after the first quarter of the eighteenth century, when the colonists' "mimetic" impulses reached their zenith, did New Englanders travel to England and other parts of Europe to receive a professional medical education.[58] Thus the only elite practitioners to exert any influence on clerical healers were a loosely affiliated group of iatrochemical physicians in New England. Without the benefit of orthodox medical training and professional organizations such as the Royal College of Physicians and the Royal Society to inform and influence medical beliefs, medicine in New England followed a path of development which deviated from its path in the mother country. Iatrochemical texts became the medical authorities for many of the educated elite practitioners. The texts were supplemented by correspondence between such famous colonial healers as Winthrop and Bulkeley and the Puritan chemical reformers of England. Galenic medicine, as incorporated into the dispensatories of Nicholas Culpeper and William Salmon, so widely collected by the colonists, was not supplanted by iatrochemical medicine; rather, Galenism continued to influence popular as well as professional medicine well into the nineteenth century.

Another factor which may have led to the popularity of the overtly religious iatrochemical treatises among these divines may be surmised from the paucity in their personal libraries of Cartesian and other texts on the mechanical philosophy. Only two of the collections surveyed, those of Samuel Lee (Oxford M.A., 1648) and Samuel Brackenbury (HC 1664), contained the works of Descartes.[59] By the latter part of the seventeenth century, Cartesianism and other variants of the mechanical philosophy had gained a stronghold among many European scientists. However, the development of a mechanistic world view in turn gave rise to criticism of the materialistic, atheistic implications of the doctrine. An "inevitable backlash," including a retreat into the deeply religious doctrines of Neoplatonism, hermeticism, and alchemy, followed.[60] Although Charles Morton's "Compendium Physicae" provided Harvard students with explanations of Cartesian theory from 1687 through 1717, it apparently took time for Harvard students to develop an interest in the new mechanical philosophy. A particular fascination with iatrochemistry (as well as hermeticism and Neoplatonism) has been discerned among the New England clerics investigated in the present study. Only in the Revolutionary decades do the collections of preacher-physicians and regular physicians begin to reflect an interest in the mechanical theories of Newton and the accompanying iatromechanism they spawned.

Although the physical sciences came to be stressed over medical chemistry at Harvard and alchemical works gradually lost their appeal to the New England clergy during the first half of the eighteenth century, preacher-physicians continued to prescribe chemical therapies for their patients with great regularity. As late as 1754, Gershom Bulkeley's grandson, the minister-physician Richard Treat, billed a patient in Colchester, Connecticut, for such items as "red precipitate," "antimony," and "Rubila," the celebrated alchemical remedy formulated by John Winthrop, Jr.[61] Chemical medicines such as these had become firmly entrenched in the American arsenal against disease; they are found interspersed with herbal Galenic and folk remedies and charges for the "bleeding" of patients, in the clerical and lay medical account books that have survived from the eighteenth century. Emphasis came to be placed on the degree to which a particular remedy appeared to be effective, based on repeated trials, with little regard given to whether the agent used was chemically prepared or herbal. J. Worth Estes suggests that both Galenic and iatrochemical medical practices were used by regular physicians, and that the usage of the two eventually fused in the minds of practitioners.[62] It would appear that, for ministers practicing medicine as well as for regular doctors, as interest in the mystical aspects of iatrochemical theory waned, the practical side of chemical therapeutics was retained alongside other forms of therapy.

Chapter 5

Anatomy and Surgery

The 1749 inventory of the estate of the Reverend Benjamin Doolittle (YC 1706) of Northfield, Massachusetts, contains "a surgeon's pocket case of instruments," valued at twenty-two pounds; "three sets of instruments to extract teeth," at one pound and five shillings; "two lancets" at twenty-four shillings; and "an incision-knife" at eight shillings. These implements strongly suggest that Doolittle performed some surgical procedures on his parishioners. He also acted as both surgeon and physician in the military, as a debt from "the King for medicine for the Canada Soldiers" in the amount of "229.18s.5d." was still owed to his estate after his death.[1] A number of the minister-physicians in this study practiced procedures within the realm of the surgeon, both during military service and at home upon their parishioners. A survey of these clerics' libraries indicates that roughly a third collected surgical texts. Anatomical studies were even more popular among the clergy, with approximately two-thirds owning works on this subject. An exploration of the clergymen's knowledge and practice of surgical procedures, in addition to their understanding of the related field of anatomy, sheds light on the breadth of the minister's healing role in colonial society. In addition, such a study also illuminates the attitudes of these Puritan divines toward such invasive and bloody procedures as autopsy. Clerical surgical practices and anatomical studies are here compared to those of lay practitioners, to help determine to what degree the ministers' attitudes and techniques resembled or diverged from those of the lay group, and how the former may have changed throughout the colonial period.

In preparing his "Admirable Secrets of Physick and Chirurgery" late in the seventeenth century, the Reverend Thomas Palmer revealed that he had "seen and read many authors, the best part of thirty." His *vade mecum* refers to a number of surgical procedures, including the treatment of wounds, ulcers, "cancers" and fractures. The surgical texts upon which he relied for guidance were John Woodall's *The Surgions Mate* (1617) and James Cooke's *Mellificium Chirurgiae, or the Marrow of Chirurgery* (1626). Both works were written in plain, simple English, probably were intended for the poorly educated surgeon's mate, and were quite popular in England during the seventeenth century. Invoices sent from London to the Boston booksellers John Foy and John Usher in the second half of the seventeenth century reveal that Cooke's works were available to the colonists. It is not unlikely that Rev. Palmer obtained his copy from one of them.[2]

On the eve of the colonization of New England, John Woodall had become a leading spokesman for English surgeons, who increasingly were invading the professional realms of the apothecaries, barbers, and physicians, resulting in the proliferation of general practitioners in both London and the provinces. There had never been enough "pure" surgery to support this group, so they often performed blood-letting, which officially was the responsibility of the barbers, as well as a fair degree of internal medicine, traditionally within the physician's realm. John Woodall, whose *Surgions Mate* addressed the practice of surgery and medicine at sea, argued that "no Doctors will serve in his [Majesty's] Nauye and therefore ther is a necessitye of their [the surgeons] being licensed to practize phisicke." The surgeons were probably the first group of English practitioners to administer the new mineral and chemical therapies associated with the school of Paracelsus to their patients, especially in the case of syphilis. As early as the sixteenth century, surgeons had argued that such new diseases as syphilis necessitated the use of novel forms of treatment which could not be relegated entirely to the realm of either the surgeon, who treated localized conditions, or the physician, who practiced internal medicine. Many surgeons continued to give internal medications like guaiacum in cases of venereal diseases, as an adjunct to external treatment with mercurial preparations. Thus, in some cases it was impossible, in the minds of many surgeons, to separate internal medicine from the treatment of what were considered external conditions. The surgeon increasingly functioned as general practitioner, much against the wishes of the Royal College of Physicians. It was absurd, of course, for the college to pretend that some forty physicians could provide adequate health care to a city of over 300,000. With the outbreak of Civil War shortly after the colonization of New England, all forms of authority became suspect, and the college-educated physicians did not even attempt to impede the proliferation of the general practitioner in London or the provinces. Not surprisingly, the same situation prevailed in New England, where the general practitioner, whether cleric or layman, was the most prevalent type of healer, often performing both internal treatments and minor surgical procedures, as well as compounding drugs.[3]

One-fifth of the ministers' collections surveyed contained the surgical manuals of James Cooke (see table 3.1), an ardent Puritan who had gained much of his experience in surgery in Cromwell's army. It is not surprising that Boston booksellers chose to import the text of a Puritan surgeon rather than those of Richard Wiseman, Royal Surgeon to Charles II, whose *Several Chirurgical Treatises* (1672) gained him the reputation as the father of English surgery.[4] Rev. Palmer included a number of passages from Cooke's *Marrow of Chirurgery* in the surgical sections of his *vade mecum*. From Cooke he learned the procedures for amputation in the presence of gangrene, and, when he observed the "Corruption of Bones," he learned to "Bare the bone by incision, Caustick, or dilation." Cooke had instructed him to recognize four sorts of "Flesh discoloured" which required surgical attention, namely "Red, Yellow, Livid or black. Red proceeds from heat, or by blood offending in quality or quantity." In this case he would "first bleed & Scarrify the part & apply Leeches." If his patient had "Black" flesh, the cause could be from "heat or could. If from heat, an inflammation went before it. If from cold, lividity did proceed." In both of these cases, "the parts are to be scarrified profoundly, using a Lixiv[ium]," a lye solution to which Palmer added a variety of herbs. He would then "fill the incision of the Scarification" with a combination of lye and a meal made of beans, barley and maple bark until the color of the flesh (somewhat miraculously) "returns to the Natural Colour." Palmer explained the etiology of conditions requiring surgery in Galenic terms, yet he often recommended the use of "fixed salts of vegitables" (prepared according to the precepts of Paracelsian theory) for their treatment. Palmer would place these fixed salts "into an old or ulcerate soar, [which] doth cleanse it to admiration & procure good quitter [i.e., pus]. . . . Though it be very painful it makes sweet a stinking soar & is far more safe then Arsenick . . . & can do no hurt though others may." Colonial surgeons favored the (erroneous) Galenic notion that the promotion of supporation, or "laudable pus" as it was often called, stimulated the healing of the wound.[5]

Clerical records reveal that various forms of what was thought to be cancer, particularly cancer of the breast, were frequently diagnosed in colonial times. The English surgeon Richard Wiseman recommended amputation in the case of breast cancer, and afterwards he would secure "the artery by the touch of the hot iron." James Cooke also recommended that "if in the Breast there be little hard Tumors, they are to bee taken out as Cancers, and cured according to Art."[6] Rev. Palmer defined cancer as

a hard unequal round venemous humour, blackish of Colour, . . . bred of burnt choler. The humour is salt in taste. It may grow in any part of the body, especially in . . . womens brests . . . & it is hardly cured. Inward cancers admit no cure, nor those that are inveterate, unless they be cured by incision or burning. . . . It must be salved out, burnt out, or cut out by the roots. . . . Cut it wholly away with an incision knife, presse the thick blood out of the Veines nere to it that [it] may flow forth again, joyn the lips of the ulcer togeth[er] & go forward to cure it as other ulcers. Some consume it with a Cautery; with Caustick Medicine it may be done . . . with arsenic sublimate, used warily.[7]

While Palmer's records indicate that he may have performed some surgery for cancer, he obviously was wary of such endeavours, and, in the case of breast cancer, he admitted that it was "hardly cured." While it is nearly impossible to determine if these were ulcers or cancers, a number of ministers who treated what was diagnosed as "cancer" often applied herbal mixtures to the site affected rather than resort to the harsher, riskier procedure of amputation or the excision of a tumor. The Reverend Ebenezer Parkman acquired a remedy for "an Excellent Drink ag[ain]st a *Cancer*" from John Hunt, Esq., which was composed of "Dock Root, Elder Root, Succory Root– steeped in whey." He had another from "Dr. Simon," who had gotten it from "Mr. Peabody," which included "Cancer Herb." Parkman bathed the affected area of his patient with the liquid mixture, and also administered it internally. If the sore was "raw," then he would "dip a piece of muslin and lay [it] on ye sore & dry some of ye root [cancer herb]; pulveriz it fine, [and] blow it on with a Quill." He also recommended applying "Culpeper's Tobacco Ointment," and, in the case of "a Cancerous Humour in the Lip," he used oyster shell and allum powder mixed in vinegar, a remedy he received from "D.R. Blower of Beverly" with her or his highest praise. Parkman apparently was widely recognized for his efforts to cure cancer.

In his diary, Parkman reveals that it was not uncommon for out-of-towners to see him for advice on a cure. On 8 May 1752, he recorded that "Mr. Joseph Sever of Framingham came to me about the Cancer in his Leg, that he might know how to use Mechoacan or Poke Weed." Parkman evidently had become involved in a public controversy over cancer remedies; the 18 February 1752 edition of the *Boston Gazette* contained a note by him which claimed that at New Haven he "*made a Business of discoursing with Capt. Dickerman; who told him, it was* Mechoacan *that he used for his Cancer in his Cheek.*" A man by the name of Benevolentius replied in a later edition that Parkman was wrong about this cure, and a heated debate between the two over the proper cure for cancer continued in the *Boston Gazette*, a valuable source of medical and surgical information for the reading public throughout the eighteenth century. This controversy only served to strengthen his reputation as a minister knowledgeable in the treatment of cancers.[8]

In the same vein, Cotton Mather's *Angel of Bethesda*, intended for public consumption, recommended "Turnips boil'd, and made unctuous with a little fresh *Hogslard*" in the case of "*Hard Swellings* in Womens *Breasts*." The "Old Medicine of the *London-midwives* to break and heal Sore Breasts," contained oatmeal, sage, honey, and Venice-Turpentine applied as a "plaister."[9] Apparently the minister did not avoid that area of medicine which in England was often left to the midwives. In addition, much like the ministers' exchange of Galenic and chemical remedies for internal disease, remedies for the condition known to colonials as cancer were widely traded, collected, and published for use by the public.

Lay physicians appear to have used remedies for cancer and other conditions within the surgeon's realm much like those of the ministry. The physician and surgeon of Salem, Zerobabel Endecott (c. 1635–84), son of Gov. John Endecott, put together a collection of remedies in 1677 which recommended the use of tobacco ointments "to Cure Tumors Aposthums wounds Ulcers Gun shot botches Scabs Itch Stinging with Nettles, Bees, wasps, hornets . . . wounds made with poysoned Arrows . . . it helps . . . burnings though with Lightning & that without scar[ring,] it helpeth nasty Rotten stinking putrifyed Ulcers though in the Legs, . . . [where] the humours are most subject to resort." He reported the case of a woman from Casko Bay, Maine, who "had a Cancer in her breast which after much menes used in vaine they aplyed strong beer to it . . . which it [the cancer] drank in very Greedyly & was something eased afterwards." When the beer failed to cure her, rum was used "in Like manner which seemed to Lull it a sleep;" they then "put Arsnik into it & dressing it twice a day was Parfactly whol." However, "in the meane time har kind husband by Su[c]king drewe har brest with ye Losse of his Fore teeth without any farther hurt."[10] If the *National Enquirer* had been published in the seventeenth century, it certainly would have paid dearly for this story.

The Reverend Eli Forbes (HC 1751) attempted to cure what he had diagnosed as breast cancer in his wife, but, being unable to do so, he took her to "Mr. Pope," a physician in Boston. Many of the ministers in this study would call in a regular physician to treat members of their family when their efforts failed. The doctor used various "hard plaisters" on her breast rather than attempt surgical removal, but she died of the tumor several months later. His next wife also suffered from what Forbes thought was cancer, and he received some encouragement when he used "dock root" to treat her. Yet she too fell victim to the disease, even though her husband had spent three years battling it.[11]

Although Cotton Mather reported in his *Angel of Bethesda*, which he composed in the early 1720s, that the "Manual Operation [for the removal of bladder stones] is now with much success very commonly practised," he personally recommended a number of herbal cures for the disorder. In fact, although lithotomy was performed as a last resort in Europe, it was rarely attempted in the colonies. Judging from the records of the ministers, as well as of lay physicians and surgeons, serious surgical procedures (such as amputation) were performed only as a last resort. And in the case of what the ministers diagnosed as cancer (which may or may not have been the disease as we know it today), they nearly uniformly relied upon herbal cures rather than attempting to remove the tumor surgically, as was recommended by such expert English surgeons as Cooke and Wiseman. The seventeenth century, a pre-antiseptic age before the development of anesthesia, was not known for great advances in surgery. Surgeons continued to lance boils, set bones, and treat wounds with various ointments and washes. Ministers performed such minor procedures as tooth-drawing and the treatment of wounds but apparently shied away from more serious procedures. For example, an examination of the medical account books of the Reverend Samuel Wigglesworth (HC 1707; son of the minister-physician Michael Wigglesworth) for the period 1710–11 reveals that the only procedures he performed within the surgeon's realm were the dressing of a "sore finger" and "drawing a tooth" for Charles Tuttle of Ipswich. It is doubtful, however, that the clergy refrained from performing serious and life-threatening procedures in response to religious proscriptions; rather, they probably had seen a number of procedures performed by lay surgeons which resulted in the patient's death. In 1674, the Reverend John Eliot entered in the records of the First Church of Roxbury that he had been asked to attend "the cut[t]ing [of] b[rother] Livermores daughter of a wonderfull great timpany," a distention of the abdominal wall, but the girl unfortunately died the following day as a result of the procedure. Perhaps the parson did not want to bear on his conscience such an onerous burden as the death of a parishioner. John Duffy has suggested that regular surgeons also were equally reluctant to remove their patients from the land of the living.[12]

An interesting case recorded by Pope Innocent III in 1212 addresses the difficulties involved when a monk lost a patient after his surgical intervention:

> You asked *to be advised by the Apostolic See* what must be decided concerning a certain monk who, believing that he could cure a certain woman of a tumor of the throat, acting as a surgeon, opened the tumor with a knife. When the tumor had healed somewhat, he ordered the woman not to expose herself to the wind at all lest the wind, stealing into the incision in her throat, bring about her death. But the woman, defying his order, rashly exposed herself to the wind while gathering crops, and thus much blood flowed out through the incision in her throat, and the woman died. She, nevertheless, confessed that she was responsible because she had exposed herself to the wind. The question is whether this monk, since he is also a priest, may lawfully exercise his priestly office. We therefore reply to your brotherhood that, although the monk himself was very much at fault for usurping an alien function which very little suited him, nevertheless, if he did it from piety and not from cupidity, and was expert in the exercise of surgery and was zealous to employ every diligence which he ought to have done, he must not be condemned for that which happened through the fault of the woman against his advice. Then, with no penance required, he may be permitted to celebrate divine service. Otherwise, the fulfilling of the sacerdotal office must be strictly forbidden him.

A few years afterwards, the Fourth Lateran Council forbade subdeacons, deacons, and priests from practicing "that part of surgery involving burning and cutting," but refrained from mentioning the external treatment of wounds and sores, the setting of broken bones, the treatment of dislocations, and other aspects of surgical practice. In addition, those forms of surgery mentioned were forbidden only to those clerics who were in major orders, "who would have been most severely affected by incurring a canonical irregularity." The concern here was to prevent a cleric from performing an act which could result in the patient's death; if he did cause death, canon law would prevent him from fulfilling such spiritual functions as the hearing of confession. In surgical interventions, the risk of causing a patient's death was much greater than in the practice of medicine. Maltreatment in medical practice was relatively difficult to prove, but in the case of surgery, an active intrusion into the patient's body, it was much easier (and more common) for the death of the patient to be attributed to the surgical practitioner.[13]

Darrel Amundsen recently has explored the question of whether or not the medieval clergy were ever forbidden to practice medicine or surgery. In the official collections of universal canon law of the Middle Ages, there are four statutes which relate to the formal study of medicine and surgery by clerics, and which prohibit certain groups of clergy from leaving their religious houses to study these arts; however, they do not forbid them from practicing. It often has been claimed that the medieval Church forbade all clerics to practice surgery on the grounds that "Ecclesia abhorret a sanguine" ("the Church abhors the shedding of blood"). But as Charles Talbot has argued, this quotation is nothing more than a "literary ghost" created by Quesnay in 1774, "the uncritical historian of the Faculty of Surgery at Paris." No earlier source for this phrase can be found in canon law. Evidence indicates that medieval canon law was not nearly so restrictive on the issues of medicine and surgery as many historians have maintained.[14]

In addition to the precedent of medieval canon law barring a cleric from fulfilling his sacerdotal functions after losing a patient as a result of surgical endeavor, in Puritan New England another factor made the minister reluctant to undertake serious surgical procedures. Congregationalism was a major source of social stability in early New England, and, as patriarch of a town's congregation, the minister typically was relied upon to heal dissension within the community. The loss of a life as a result of the minister's surgical intervention certainly would have damaged his reputation and authority within the community and perhaps led to his dismissal. Other factors which may have kept a minister from pursuing surgical practice are a lack of specific training or experience and a distaste for inflicting intense pain on others.[15]

Away from the watchful eyes of the community, a number of ministers did gain practical experience treating war wounds as military surgeons. One of the most famous ministers who was inducted into the army as a surgeon during the early colonial period was Gershom Bulkeley (HC 1655). Bulkeley began studying medicine at least as early as 1661, just a few years after taking his master's degree at Harvard. During 1661, he began preaching at New London, where he was contracted as minister at a salary of eighty pounds per year for three years. Interspersed throughout his sermon notes for this year are medical remedies copied from a variety of sources, attesting to his interest in both the ministry and medicine from an early point in his professional life. An examination of his library indicates that he was also interested in the art of surgery, as he owned four works on the subject, including James Cooke's *The Marrow of Chirurgery*. It is possible that he had attained some degree of notoriety for his surgical skills during his ministry, because, with the onset of King Philip's War in 1675, the General Court of Connecticut ordered Bulkeley "to be improved in this present expedition, to be chyrurgion to our army." However, the commission of a surgeon or surgeon's mate rarely required any demonstration of competence until standards were established after the beginning of the American Revolution. Bulkeley must have served somewhat competently, however, because the army paid him thirty pounds for his services. In addition, Connecticut had outlawed the export of corn from the colony because of its scarcity, yet he was "granted liberty to transport 60 bush[els of] corn to Boston . . . to purchase som necessaries and phissicall druggs," no doubt to replenish his supplies expended during the war. Even when home in Wethersfield, "being informed that sundry wounded men are come to Mr. Buckly," the General Court desired that he would "take the care and trouble of dressing the s[ai]d wounded souldiers till God bless his endeauoures with a cure." Bulkeley's reputation was such that the wounded sought out his assistance even after he was no longer serving officially as an army surgeon.[16]

The Reverend Israel Chauncy of Stratford, Connecticut, Bulkeley's classmate at Harvard, also was engaged by the General Court as surgeon and chaplain during King Philip's War, for which he was awarded two hundred acres of land. His son Charles (HC 1686) followed in his footsteps, becoming both chaplain and physician to the Army of Connecticut in 1690–91.[17] Qualified surgeons were a rarity in pre-Revolutionary New England, and ministers such as these no doubt were selected for military service because of their social standing, which signified that they were respectable members of the community, and because of their proven ability to perform the duties of a physician as well as minister. In addition, the minister was perceived as a special "arbiter" with God, and perhaps it was thought that God "would bless his endeauores with a cure" more willingly than he would those of an uneducated lay surgeon.[18]

Rev. John Graham (YC 1740) served as both minister and surgeon throughout his life, and when he was appointed chaplain to the expedition against Havana in 1762, he poignantly recorded the devastating effects of war and disease on his men. In camp at night, he heard "bursting groans from throbbing hearts seized with panick, horror and Surprise because febrile flames kindles [*sic*] upon their vitals, or Tyrant pain, Tyger like preys upon their Bones or as a harpy Devours their entrails, forbids repose." During the day, as the men marched, they were:

> wasted with Sickness: their flesh all consumed, their bones looking thro the Skin, a Mangie and pale Countenance, Eyes almost Sunk into there heads, with a dead and downcast look – hands weak, knees feeble, Joints trembling – leaning upon Staves like men bowed and over loaded with old age . . . they slowly move along Stagger and Reel, like drunken men – pityfull Objects. . . . There is one, two, three Graves open'd, here they come with as many Corps, there blankets both there winding sheet and Coffins; scarce have they finished the interment of these, but a messenger comes in hast to tell them they must open a grave or two more.[19]

As earlier chapters have demonstrated, a minister's journal, sermons, and poetry often reveal much about his understanding of and attitudes toward medical topics. Much like the journal of Rev. Graham, with its penetrating portrayal of impotence in the face of disease and death during wartime, the Reverend Edward Taylor's poetry lucidly grapples with such concerns as death and the corruption of the body after life. In a funeral elegy on the death of the Reverend Samuel Hooker, son of the famous Thomas Hooker of Connecticut, Taylor chastised his listeners for departing from the ways of their fathers: "Be n't like such babes as parents brains out pull/ To make a Wassill Bowle then of the Skull./ That Pick their Parents eyes out, and the holes/ Stuff up with folly, as if no braind Souls." Indeed, such frank allusions to the bodies of the dead were commonplace during the colonial period, as minister and laity alike held a morbid fascination with death and physical decay, a carryover from medieval and Renaissance times. Such phraseology naturally would form part of a medical minister's lexicon.[20]

More mundane factors, such as economic motivation, also may have led some clerics to act as both chaplain and surgeon in the military. John Dennis (HC 1730) became a chaplain in the army in 1737 and was stationed at Fort Saint Georges, Richmond Fort, and Fort Frederick in Maine. In 1747, he petitioned the House of Representatives for additional compensation because he had acted "in the Capacity of a Physician and Cirurgeon." After his military career, he experienced a series of problematical ministries and dismissals, again encountering difficulty in obtaining adequate financial support. He finally quit the ministry and began teaching school in Ipswich in 1771 for ten dollars a month.[21]

Ammi Ruhamah Cutter had graduated from Harvard in the class of 1725 and shortly thereafter accepted a ministry on the frontier in Maine. His liberal, Arminian leanings soon led to his dismissal, and he was then hired by the province as physician and surgeon to the soldiers at Fort George. He became chief surgeon of the garrison at Louisburg, and his son followed in his footsteps, becoming a military surgeon, too.[22] As discussed in chapter 2, when a minister held religious views inconsistent with those of his parishioners, it could eventually force him to change his profession. Therefore, many ministers, well aware of their tenuous positions, particularly during the turbulent decades of the Great Awakening, learned medicine as well as surgery as a second occupation, in case they lost their positions.

During the eighteenth century, some Harvard and Yale graduates who intended to enter the ministry upon completing their education were unable to obtain a pulpit, and a number turned to the practice of medicine and surgery. For example, Nathaniel Bond (HC 1766) failed to receive a call and so practiced medicine in Marblehead, Massachusetts, and later became a surgeon during the American Revolution. The dramatic increase in military operations in 1741–81, a period which included the assault on Louisburg in 1745, the Seven Years War, and the American Revolution, provided many would-be ministers with surgical occupations. The demand for military surgeons was greater than the need for new ministers, leading many graduates who were sensitive to the changing needs of society to choose an alternative profession.[23]

An essential part of the minister's surgical endeavors was an understanding of human anatomy. Over two-thirds of the ministers' libraries surveyed contained anatomical textbooks (see table 3.1). Samuel Brackenbury (HC 1664) possessed one of the most up-to-date medical libraries in this group, with six anatomical works in his collection. He owned the Danish physician Thomas Bartholin's *Institutiones anatomicae* (1641) and his *Historiarium anatomicarum* (1654–61), Thomas Willis's *Cerebri anatome* (1664) and *Pathologiae cerebri, et nervosi generis specimen* (1667), Jean Riolan's *Encheiridium anatomicum, et patholigicum* (1648), and Jean Pecquet's celebrated *Experimenta nova anatomica* (1651).

The most popular anatomical texts among the New England clergy were those of Thomas Bartholin, whose works, present in 32 percent of the libraries surveyed, addressed the findings of William Harvey and were considered very up-to-date by the academic standards of the seventeenth century.[24] Another popular anatomical authority was Thomas Willis, whose works were present in roughly a third of the collections. Perhaps the most salient feature of the writings of this disciple of William Harvey was the application of his anatomical, physiological, and chemical researches to his clinical observations. Willis sought to define the relationship between the circulation of the blood and the generation of body heat, and suggested a model of explanation based on a process of chemical fermentation. Among New Englanders, his most popular work was *Cerebri anatome*, which in its time contained the most complete and accurate description of the nervous system, a status it maintained until the late eighteenth century. In this treatise, Willis rejected the Cartesian notion that the seat of the soul was in the pineal gland.[25] The catalogues of the library of Harvard in 1723 and Yale in 1743 both record the presence of Willis's works. So these anatomical texts, in addition to a number of others, were available to all students, many of whom would pursue the path of the angelical conjunction. The works of the French anatomist Jean Riolan, Jr., were present in 15 percent of the collections surveyed. He has been characterized as an "international arbiter" on the new anatomical work then being produced throughout Europe. He initially accepted but later rejected Harvey's theory of circulation because it undercut Galen's theories, to which he was devoted. Yale owned his *Opera anatomica*, and Harvard had his *Surest Guide to Physick & Surgery* (London, 1657).[26]

All three of the anatomical authors most popular among the ministers (Bartholin, Willis, and Riolan), addressed the work of William Harvey on the circulation of the blood, which is now considered one of the most important medical discoveries of the seventeenth century. Two of the ministers, Samuel Lee and Michael Wigglesworth, owned copies of Harvey's influential *Exercitatio anatomica de motu cordis* (1628), and in 1699, the minister-physician Rowland Cotton argued in favor of blood circulation for his master's degree at Harvard.

In his study of the development of medicine in America, Richard Shryock asked, "How far . . . were the first American-born generations aware of European medicine and of its latest developments? . . . few colonists seem to have been interested in the striking developments under way in English science . . . with three or four exceptions, the number of such publications in early American libraries was not impressive."[27] The above examination of clerical libraries reveals that 60 percent of the collections surveyed had works on the latest developments in anatomy and experimental physiology. Since the libraries of the Puritan clergy, arguably the best educated segment of colonial New England society, never previously have been examined from a medical perspective, it is hardly surprising that some historians have argued that the colonists existed in a medical "vacuum," lacking familiarity with European advances.

In addition to attaining a knowledge of anatomy through reading textbooks, a number of ministers gained valuable insight into the structure of human bodies through the practice of autopsy. Autopsies had been performed regularly in Europe since the Middle Ages, in order to determine the probable cause of death, and the Catholic Church did not oppose such procedures. In 1348, the city of Florence hired physicians to perform autopsies on plague victims "to know more clearly the illnesses of the bodies." Post-mortem examinations were done for instructional purposes within the universities and guilds, as well as in private practice, to determine the cause of disease, especially in cases of death in unusual or mysterious circumstances. In fact, autopsies were so routine that if a relative of the deceased forbade the procedure it was considered quite unusual. In 1486, the husband of Bartolomea Rinieri wrote that when his wife was near death from a "diseased womb," she asked him "to have her autopsied so that our daughter or others could be treated . . . I had this done, and it was found that her womb was so calcified that it could not be cut with a razor."[28] In the *New England Weekly Journal* for 2 February 1735–36, a similar account was published about Margaret Fisher of Dedham, Massachusetts. While dying of a *"Pulmonary Pthisis,"* she demonstrated *"an exemplary publick Spirit and Benevolence to Mankind* [because] . . . she earnestly desired, that her *Viscera* might be *Anatomically inspected*, for the Benefit of those, who may be afflicted with the like Disorders." At this time, attitudes towards autopsy in New England were quite positive and apparently were uninhibited by religious or social prohibitions.

An examination of church records and clerical diaries from Puritan New England reveals that the minister not uncommonly attended or performed autopsies. In April 1647, the Reverend John Fiske of Wenham, Massachusetts, recorded in his daybook a graphic description of an autopsy he had performed that day on an infant. The women who had attended the birth of "Sister Patch" had sent for the minister when her baby was stillborn, having "a head not like other children." After he, the midwife, and the other women present had examined the baby's head, they unanimously agreed that the infant's skull had been broken. However, "not so satisfied" with these findings, the minister then

> opened the head and laid the skull bare till I let out most of the jelly matter, which I had before felt and some of it consisted of brains, fibres, and blood, some congealed and some watery, so mixed as the brains and fibres could hardly be discerned for the congealed blood. . . .

Then perceiving nothing offensive in the opening of the head, I smelled it, and likewise after me the rest of the women, and we perceived no ill or corrupt savor in aught. So we left it to be seen of others.[29]

One of the interesting aspects of this account is that the minister was called in to aid the midwife, and that he asked all of the women who had attended the birth of Sister Patch to confirm his findings at every stage of the procedure. In Haverhill, the Reverend Samuel Bacheller (HC 1731) also was called in by the midwives, but, unlike the case above, during rather than after the birth. "Mr. Bacheller took the midwife's place," testified one Elizabeth Currier who had attended the birth, "and as I thought, and heard several women say, acted in a very strange manner." The women present then sent for "Dr. Howe," who "deliver'd the woman of a still-born child, which was judged to expire after the woman was in Mr. Bacheller's hands; and I heard some of the women say, they believed the woman would have died in Mr. Bacheller's hands if they had not desired him to let her alone." Again, as in the case of surgery, the reputation of a minister who engaged in this occasionally risky procedure, usually left to the midwife, could suffer irreparable damage if his endeavors were unsuccessful. Bacheller was subsequently arraigned by a council of nine New England ministers for "preaching false doctrine," and the above testimony of one of the witnesses of his unsuccessful attempts to deliver a baby to a parishioner served to damage his character.[30]

Twenty-one percent of the ministers in this study (see table 3.1) and 13 percent of the physicians surveyed collected books on midwifery, a fact that may indicate that it was not uncommon for clerics or doctors to consult and assist in such difficult births as these. In colonial Virginia, works on obstetrics were more common in the libraries of the gentry than works on general surgery; this suggests that the profession of the midwife may have been "invaded" by males earlier than previously has been thought.[31] In Massachusetts, Zerobabel Endecott's 1677 *vade mecum* on medicine and surgery contains observations on his obstetrical operations for removing a dead fetus with instruments. Endecott even developed his own obstetrical instruments: "Thare is also another [obstetrical] instrument which is to be fownd in som

Awthers & by them used which I came to make use of [which] I fownd not soe fitt nor proffitable for ye workes as I did expect which som Call a Griffins Talon with a sharp poynt but by ye good providence of God who doth designe every man to his worke & instruct them theirto & thirein also I was by my former employment [?] enabled or Instructed to mak my owne Instruments fitt for present use that was before me." Dr. John Avery, a contemporary of Endecott's, also was reputed to have "notable skill in . . . midwifery & invented some usefull instrum[en]ts for that case."[32]

In the above case of Rev. Fiske's autopsy of the stillborn infant, his tone is so matter-of-fact that it easily could be assumed that he often performed or witnessed autopsies, and that the procedure itself was commonplace. The fact that he intended to leave the infant with its brains exposed "to be seen of others" indicates that other members of the community would want to come and see the results for themselves! There is a complete absence of a religious interpretation of this stillbirth in the minister's diary. "Monstrous" births like the one reported by Gov. John Winthrop by "Mary Dier" who "brought forth . . . a woman childe, a fish, a beast, and a fowle, all woven together in one, and without an head" or the "thirty monstrous births" of Anne Hutchinson typically were interpreted as a product of "mis-shapen" religious opinions and as a result of the midwife's notoriety "for familiarity with the Devill." After the midwife confessed where the "monster" had been buried, the body of Dyer's infant was ex-humed, "and though it were much corrupted, . . . the horns, claws, and holes in the back, and some scales, & c. were found and seen of above a hundred persons."[33] Rev. Fiske's procedure, the results of which also were observed by many others, could, unlike the one Win-throp recorded, be described as purely "clinical." However, the ab-sence of a religious interpretation does not necessarily exclude the possibility that the minister was asked to examine the child to deter-mine if some supernatural cause for the death of the infant might be found, or to remove suspicion that the incompetence of the midwife had resulted in the child's death.

Another autopsy was performed by Deacon Bray Rosseter in 1662. The General Court of Connecticut paid him twenty pounds for "open-

ing Kellies child." The autopsy was performed because of the suspicion that "Goody Ayres" had bewitched Kelly's daughter, causing her
to sicken and die. The post-mortem report lists "6 particulars" which
Rosseter judged "preternatural," which the modern reader might at-
tribute to the decomposition of the corpse; the child died on the 26th
of March, and the autopsy was performed on the 31st of March.[34]

Suspicion of witchcraft and fear of the supernatural were not the
only reasons for conducting autopsies in colonial New England. If an
inquiry pointed to the possibility of foul play, a body might be opened
to determine if the victim were murdered. In addition, as Renaissance
reports have shown, the body often was opened to determine the
pathology of the disease process. During the plague epidemic of 1665,
the Reverend John Allin (who had graduated from Harvard in 1643
and removed to England) explained that a number of his fellow-
practitioners who were iatrochemists "would give money for the most
infected body they could heare of to dissect, which [th]ey had, and
opened to search the seate of this disease."[35] Although Paracelsus himself was no ardent supporter of anatomical research, his belief that
diseases were discrete entities rather than a product of the imbalanced
humors actually may have stimulated anatomical investigation among
chemical practitioners such as these. And, as chapter 4 has demonstrated, a number of the ministers in this study actively pursued the
study of iatrochemistry, which may have fueled their interest in post-
mortem examination.

Colonial church records often provide graphic descriptions of autopsies attended by the local minister. In the records of the First Church
of Roxbury for 1674, the Reverend Samuel Danforth wrote that John
Bridge had died of the "Winde Collick; His body was opened. He
had sundry small holes in his stomak & bowels, & one hole in his
stomak . . . [that] a mans fist might passe through."[36] Cotton Mather's
sister Katherine died when she was an infant, after a sickness of four
or five months. He recorded in his diary that "when she was opened,
it was found, that the right lobe of her lungs was utterly wasted." And
when his own son Joseph lived only four days after birth, his body
too was "opened" to determine the cause. J. Worth Estes recently has
discovered nearly seventy-five colonial autopsy reports, suggesting

that this was a relatively mundane procedure. No doubt the minister gained practical anatomical and perhaps pathological information from post-mortem exams. Also, the procedure demonstrated to the family that the death of a loved one was not due to the practitioner's negligence, but was a natural outcome of the disease process. Cotton Mather, who displayed considerable knowledge of contemporary anatomy in the *Angel* (which is not surprising, because he owned anatomical works by Bartholin, Riolan, de Graaf, and du Laurens), tacitly implied approval of post-mortem examinations by his matter-of-fact tone in reporting the findings of such procedures throughout his diary, and by the fact that he allowed his own children to be autopsied.[37]

The above examination of the autopsies conducted and/or witnessed by the clergy provides strong evidence that there was little or no "warfare of science with theology" in early New England. The Puritans attempted to distinguish between natural and preternatural diseases through post-mortem exams; one could even assert, in light of the fear of Satan and bewitchment which was so prominent in seventeenth-century New England, that religion actually functioned as a stimulus for clinical investigation during this period. In addition, clerical records reveal that autopsies commonly were performed during this time to "search the seate of disease," disproving the recent statement by one historian of early medical education in the colonies that, although "anatomy was central to the study of medicine . . . autopsies were rarely requested or approved and bodies for dissection were very difficult to secure."[38]

In addition to his role in performing and witnessing autopsies, a minister also may have had the opportunity to witness the dissection of a cadaver purely for instructional purposes. After moving to London, the minister John Allin reported that he had spent three days "upon an anatomie" while studying physick in London.[39] And in New England, Rev. John Eliot lamented the fact that students of medicine were "forced to fall to practise before ever they saw an Anatomy made, or duly trained up in making experiments, for we never had but one Anatomy in the Countrey, which Mr. Giles Firmin . . . did make and read upon very well."[40] Firmin was a church deacon and physician as well as a surgeon who had received his medical education at Cambridge; as discussed in chapter 2, he later became a minister-physician in England. Although historians are aware of only one dissection for instructional purposes in colonial New England, the Massachusetts Body of Liberties of 1641 prohibited that the dead "be unburied twelve hours unless it be in case of anatomy." And in 1647, the same year as Eliot's letter describing Firmin's dissection, the General Court recommended, "We conceive it very necessary . . . [that] such as studies phisick or chirurgery may have liberty to reade anotomy, & to anotomize once in foure yeares some malefactor, in case there be such as the Courte shall alow of."[41] Thus the attitudes of the magistrates on such procedures as autopsy mirrored those of the clergy, as so often was the case during the seventeenth century in New England.

Samuel Brackenbury (HC 1664) had preached for a number of years at Rowley and also was a popular physician who attended Samuel Sewall and his family. In Sewall's diary for 2 September 1676, he entered, "Spent the day from 9 in the M[orning] with Mr. Brackenbury . . . dissecting the middlemost of the Indian executed the day before." One of the physicians participating took the cadaver's heart in his hand and "affirmed it to be the stomack," placing in doubt the actual level of anatomical knowledge among some lay practitioners.[42] This dissection of the body of a criminal implies that Firmin's anatomy probably was not the only one done for instructional purposes in colonial New England and that at least one individual known to exhibit the angelical conjunction attended the procedure.

During the eighteenth century, physicians increasingly attended the dissections of criminals. Dr. William Clark (HC 1726), an early member of the first Boston Medical Society (which existed from 1735-c. 1741), recorded the activities of the society in the dissection of executed criminals and the use of their bones to make "beautiful Skeletins." In 1773, the Reverend Benjamin Stillman, a Baptist considered uneducated by a number of Congregationalists, clashed with a number of Harvard students who had obtained the bodies of executed criminals for dissection. Stillman had converted a condemned criminal to the

Baptist faith just before his execution and afterwards made off with
the body across the Boston Harbor to prevent the pursuing Harvard
students from obtaining it for dissection.[43]

Colonial records indicate that such procedures as anatomical dissection became more and more common with the emergence of medicine as a distinct profession in the middle decades of the eighteenth
century. With Harvard students increasingly choosing the medical
profession over that of the ministry during these decades (see chapter 2),
it is hardly surprising that medical students, apprentices, and physicians, rather than clergymen, performed the dissection of human
bodies. Throughout the British colonies of North America during
the 1760s, as the desire to replicate and mimic British society gained
momentum, interest in improving the quality and standards of medical education grew. Many thought that one of the major defects in
the apprenticeship system, through which a large majority of colonials received their medical and surgical training, was the shortage of
cadavers for dissection. Therefore three of New England's most highly
skilled surgeons performed public dissections and lectured on anatomy. By this time, however, public disaffection with the procedure
resulted in a mob's making off with one subject, much as Rev. Stillman had done a few decades earlier. This disaffection did not deter
a group of Harvard students in the late 1760s from forming their own
semisecret "Anatomical Club," known as the "Spunks" or "Spunkers."[44]

David Stannard argues that, in New England during this period, attitudes towards death had altered dramatically, shifting away from a
severe and grim view toward a much more romantic, optimistic, and
sentimental view of death. By the middle decades of the eighteenth
century, cherubs had replaced the grim death's head motif on tomb-
stones,[45] providing evidence that New Englanders were becoming increasingly sentimental about the corpse itself. Such a change would
have made them more likely to keep physicians and medical students
from "assaulting" the bodies of their loved ones with such invasive
and mutilating procedures as autopsy and dissection.

The presence of surgical and anatomical texts in the libraries of
many of New England's minister-physicians strengthens the conjec-

ture that some performed minor surgical procedures on their parishioners or more serious operations as military surgeons, and that interest in anatomy and autopsy was widespread among this group. The
clergy typically performed only such minor procedures as tooth-
extraction and the dressing of wounds for their flocks and preferred
gentler, less invasive, and less life-threatening forms of medical treatment, such as the application of herbal medicines in the case of "cancer"
or in the treatment of wounds. One factor limiting a minister's surgical intervention may have been a fear of damaging his reputation in
the community and perhaps jeopardizing a fairly stable occupation.
A number of ministers did gain more varied and valuable experience
in the military, away from the watchful eyes of the parish. In fact,
with the marked increase in colonial military operations after 1740,
a number of Harvard and Yale graduates who failed to obtain a pulpit
entered the military as surgeons, as did a number of ministers whose
religious ideologies failed to mesh with those of their parishioners.
As New England society grew more diverse in its religious, political,
and economic ideologies in the decades preceding the Revolution, a
demand arose for more specialized medical practitioners. As practitioners of medicine and surgery organized into a profession distinct
from divinity by the mid-eighteenth century,[46] these fields of study
became more attractive career choices for many who in earlier generations would have chosen divinity.

Epilogue

In a fast-day sermon delivered to his congregation in Ipswich, Massachusetts, in 1755, the minister-physician Samuel Wigglesworth told of raging "epidemical Diseases" that were approaching the community. The explanation for the pestilence was theological:

> Health and Sickness are at his Command: If He speaks the Word, a destroying Angel shall draw his Sword against a populous City or Nation, and a pestilential Disease shall come, and sweep Multitudes into the Grave; and soon again he can say, It is enough, put up thy Sword; and Life and Health shall presently resume their Reign.[1]

While this sermon explains epidemic disease as a product of divine will, gone is the language of earlier jeremiads which pinpointed the sins of the people as the underlying cause for God's anger. And when Thomas Robie (HC 1708), a preacher heralded as New England's first scientist, published an account of his observation of an *aurora borealis*, his work was devoid of seventeenth-century-style prognostications cataloguing the manifestations of God's wrath likely to follow such unusual illumination. A disciple of Newtonian physics, Robie argued that "no Man should fright himself by supposing that dreadful things" would follow this beautiful display of natural light, "such as Famine, Sword or Sickness."

In Europe and America, a subtle shift was taking place in the ways that people conceived of God's role in the natural world. With the rise of deism and Newtonianism during the Enlightenment, the working of His will was explained as natural law rather than as God's direct intervention.[2]

The power of Puritan social institutions and the clergy's hegemony both had declined considerably by the Revolutionary era. When sickness struck, many increasingly relied upon the opinions and services of members of the burgeoning medical profession. With the emergence of New England as a modern, diversified, secular society, the minister's interpretation of disease in theological terms no longer was seen as a necessary way of understanding it. And, congruently, ministers had grown less inclined to explain illness as a product of personal and collective sin.

By the middle decades of the eighteenth century, with the proliferation of medicine as a profession distinct from divinity, many cleric-physicians found it difficult to compete with lay practitioners. When the regularly trained physician Joseph Boyden moved to Gardner, Massachusetts, in 1792, the Reverend Jonathan Osgood's own medical practice fell off considerably, forcing him to relocate to another community where he once again could generate an income from his medical practice.[3] Although the issue of salary as a point of contention between the minister and his community has been explored by a number of scholars, clerical dependence on medical practice for an income illuminates the minister's increasing involvement in worldly pursuits over the colonial period, and may indicate how New England divines were transformed "from Puritan to Yankee" in much the same fashion as the laity. As lay physicians organized and attempted to raise the standards of training and service, [4] the profession of medicine became increasingly attractive to ministers disenchanted with the uncertainty and loss of status which plagued their profession.

Although the angelical conjunction declined considerably by the middle of the eighteenth century, the minister-physician did not disappear altogether. In the other colonies of British America, high-profile religious figures perpetuated this tradition. In Pennsylvania, the Lutheran patriarch from Germany, the Reverend Henry Muhlenberg, captured some of the less pleasant aspects of the minister's medical role when he compared himself to a "privy to which all those with loose bowels came running from all directions to relieve themselves." Fortunately for his parishioners, his medical training in Europe provided him with the skills necessary to handle such complaints.[5]

In the middle colonies, two of the chief founders of Methodism,

John Wesley and Francis Asbury, provided medical care to the sick on a regular basis. Wesley's book, *Primitive Physick* (1747), went through over two dozen American editions. This immensely popular self-help medical handbook advocated primitive healing techniques which paralleled Wesley's understanding of the primitive or apostolic church. The remedies in it were simple and inexpensive, much like Wesley's concept of God's free grace. Clerical medicine persisted into the nineteenth century, with Protestant missionaries often acquiring medical skills so that they could aid the sick in remote parts of the world.[6]

While a good deal of scholarship has focused on relationships between religious systems and medical beliefs in both the Western and Eastern traditions, many issues remain unclear. For New England, in particular, a better understanding of the parallels and divergences between clerical and lay perceptions of health and healing could be gleaned from a thorough examination of lay diaries and correspondence. Very little is known, either, about the medical beliefs and practices of New England healers outside the realm of regular medicine, including bonesetters, midwives, and cunning folk. In the present study, hints at the relationship between these individuals and the colonial clergy have been teased from scanty resources, but much more work needs to be done to bring these important caregivers to life. In addition, comparisons of the case of New England with the other colonies of British North America would add to our growing understanding of the pre-Revolutionary era.[7]

Appendix 1

Preacher-Physicians

The ministers who practiced medicine and who were selected for this study all lived in New England during the colonial period. The majority of their lives were spent in Massachusetts or Connecticut, the Puritan stronghold of the New World. The following list of 126 preacher-physicians is divided into seven groups. Group 1 represents all ministers who immigrated from England during the Great Migration, as well as those ministers who entered their professional lives in the years 1630–50. Group 2 is composed of clergymen who entered their professional lives in 1651–70, Group 3 in 1671–90, Group 4 in 1691–1710, Group 5 in 1711–30, Group 6 in 1731–50, and Group 7 in 1751–70. Data provided includes dates of birth and death; place of death; and college attended, with the year the Bachelor of Arts degree was awarded (HC is Harvard College, YC is Yale College, OU is Oxford University, and CU is Cambridge University). An additional group, called "Removed to England," moved to England on a permanent basis. They are referred to occasionally in the book, but they are not included in the statistical analyses reported in chapter 2.

Group 1: 1630–1650 (N=14)

Charles Chauncy (1592–1672)
  d. Cambridge, Mass.; CU 1613
Samuel Danforth, Sr. (1626–1674)
  d. Roxbury, Mass.; HC 1643
Henry Dunster (1609–1658/9)
  d. Scituate, Mass.; CU 1630
John Eliot (1604–1690)
  d. Roxbury, Mass.; CU 1629

John Fiske (1606–1676/7)
  d. Chelmsford, Mass.; CU 1628
Thomas Hooker (1586–1647)
  d. Hartford, Conn.; CU 1607
William Hubbard (1621–1704)
  d. Ipswich, Mass.; HC 1642
John Oxenbridge (1608–1674)
  d. Boston, Mass., OU 1628

Ralph Partridge (1579–1658)
  d. Duxbury, Mass.; CU 1599
Ezekial Rogers (1590–1660/1)
  d. Rowley, Mass.; CU 1604
Thomas Thacher (1620–1678)
  d. Boston, Mass.

Thomas Thornton (1609–1700/1)
  d. Boston, Mass.; CU 1623
John Ward (1606–1693)
  d. Haverhill, Maine; CU 1628
John Wilson, Jr. (1621–1691)
  d. Medfield, Mass.; HC 1642

Group 2: 1650–1670 (N=12)

Samuel Brackenbury (1645/6–1678)
  d. Rowley, Mass.(?); HC 1664
Gershom Bulkeley (c.1636–1713)
  d. Wethersfield, Conn.; HC
1655
Barnabas Chauncy (1637–1675)
  d. Saco, Maine; HC 1657
Elnathan Chauncy (c.1639–c.1684)
  d. Barbados; HC 1661
Israel Chauncy (1644–1702/3)
  d. Stratford, Conn.; HC 1661
Nathaniel Chauncy (1681–1756)
  d. Durham, Conn.; HC 1661

Leonard Hoar (1630–1675)
  d. Boston, Mass.; HC 1650
Thomas Mayhew, Jr.
(1620/1–1657)
  d. At sea, res. Edgartown, Mass.
Phillip Nelson (c.1653–1691)
  d. At sea, res. Rowley, Mass.;
  HC 1654
James Noyes (1640–1719)
  d. Stonington, Conn.; HC 1659
John Rogers (1630–1684)
  d. Cambridge, Mass.; HC 1649
Michael Wigglesworth (1631–1705)
  d. Malden, Mass.; HC 1651

Group 3: 1671–1690 (N=11)

James Bayley (1650–1707)
  d. Roxbury, Mass.; HC 1669
William Brattle (1662–1717)
  d. Cambridge, Mass.; HC 1680
Samuel Danforth, Jr. (1666–1727)
  d. Roxbury, Mass.; HC 1683
Cotton Mather (1663–1728)
  d. Boston, Mass.; HC 1678
James Minot (1653–1735)
  d. Concord, Mass.; HC 1675
James Pierpont (1659–1714)
  d. New Haven, Conn.; HC 1681

James Sherman (1645–1718)
  d. Sudbury, Mass.(?)
Edward Taylor (1642–1729)
  d. Westfield, Mass.; HC 1671
Peter Thacher (1651–1727)
  d. Salem, Mass.; HC 1671
Joseph Webb (?)
  d. Unknown; HC 1684
John Wilson, 3rd (1660–1728)
  d. Braintree, Mass.

Group 4: 1691–1710 (N=15)

Hugh Adams (1676–1748)
  d. Durham, N.H.; HC 1697
Richard Billings (1675–1748)
  d. Little Compton, R.I.; HC
  1698
John Bulkeley (1679–1731)
  d. Colchester, Conn.; HC 1699
Charles Chauncy (1668–1714)
  d. Stratfield, Conn.; HC 1686
Benjamin Colman (1673–?)
  d. Boston, Mass.; HC 1692
Phineas Fiske (1682–1738)
  d. Haddam, Conn.; YC 1704
Daniel Greenleaf (1679/80–1763)
  d. Newbury, Mass.; HC 1696
Robert Hale (1668–1718/9)
  d. Beverly, Mass.; HC 1686

Joseph Lord (1672–1748)
  d. Chatham, Mass.; HC 1691
Thomas Palmer (c.1666–1743)
  d. Middleborough, Mass.
Anthony Stoddard (1678–1760)
  d. Woodbury, Conn.; HC 1697
Thomas Symmes (?)
  d. Unknown; HC 1698
Christopher Toppan (1671–1747)
  d. Newbury, Mass.; HC 1691
Nicholas Webster (1673–1717)
  d. Gloucester, Mass.; HC 1695
Nathaniel Williams (1675–1737/8)
  d. Boston, Mass.; HC 1695

Group 5: 1711–1730 (N=23)

John Avery (1685/6–1754)
  d. Truro, N.H.; HC 1706
Samuel Barrett (1700–1772)
  d. Hopkinton, Mass.(?); HC
  1721
Gen. William Brattle (1706–1776)
  d. Halifax, Nova Scotia; HC
  1722
Ezra Carpenter (1698/9–1785)
  d. Walpole, Mass.; HC 1720
Timothy Collins (1699–1777)
  d. Litchfield, Conn.; YC 1717
Ammi Ruhammah Cutter
  (1705–1746)
  d. Louisburg, Canada; HC 1725
Benjamin Doolittle (1695–1748/9)
  d. Northfield, Mass.; YC 1716
Jared Eliot (1685–1763)
  d. Killingworth, Conn.; YC 1706

Benjamin Fessenden (1701–1746)
  d. Sandwich, Mass.; HC 1718
John Graham (1694–1774)
  d. Southbury, Conn.; Glasgow,
  1714
Thomas Green (1699–1773)
  d. Leicester, Mass.
Elisha Mix (1705–1739)
  d. Wethersfield, Conn.(?); YC
  1724
Ebenezer Parkman (1703–1782)
  d. Westborough, Mass.; HC
  1721
James Pierpont, Jr. (1699–1776)
  d. New Hampshire; YC 1718
Thomas Robie (1688/9–1741)
  d. Salem, Mass.(?); HC 1708
Samuel Seabury (1706–1764)
  d. Hempstead, Conn.; HC 1724

Thomas Smith (1701/2–1795)
 d. Falmouth, Maine; HC 1720
Richard Treat (1694–c. 1757)
 d. Sheffield, Mass.; YC 1719
David Turner (1693–1757)
 d. Rehoboth, Mass.; HC 1718
John Walton (?–1764)
 d. unknown; YC 1720

Samuel Wigglesworth (1688/9–1768)
 d. Hamilton, Mass.; HC 1707
John Williams (1706–1774)
 d. Sharon, Conn.; HC 1725
Dudley Woodbridge (1705–1790)
 d. Stonington, Conn.; HC 1724

Group 6: 1731–1750 (N=29)

John Adams (1725–1792)
 d. Newfield, Mass.; HC 1745
Ephraim Avery (1713–1754)
 d. Mortlake, Conn.; HC 1731
Samuel Bacheller (1707–1796)
 d. unknown; HC 1731
Moses Bartlett (1707/8–1766)
 d. Portland, Conn.; YC 1730
Samuel Breck (1723–1764)
 d. Springfield, Mass.; HC 1742
Isaac Browne (1708/9–1787)
 d. Annapolis, Nova Scotia; YC 1729
Samuel Cobb (1716/7–1781)
 d. Tolland, Conn.; HC 1737
John Crocker (1722–1815)
 d. Richmond, Mass.; HC 1743
John Dennis (1708–1804)
 d. Ipswich, Mass.; HC 1730
Ebenezer Gay (1718–1796)
 d. Suffield, Conn.; HC 1737
John Graham, Jr. (1722–1796)
 d. W. Suffield, Conn.; YC 1740
Ebenezer Hinsdale (1706–1763)
 d. Vernon, Vt.; HC 1727
Ivory Hovey (1714–1803)
 d. Manomet, Mass.; HC 1735
Stephen Huse (1702–1783)
 d. Haverhill, Mass.; HC 1726
Joseph Lamson (1718–1773)
 d. Fairfield, Conn.; YC 1741

Joseph Manning (1706–1745)
 d. Woburn, Mass.; HC 1730
Timothy Mix (1711–1779)
 d. New Haven, Conn.; YC 1731
Ebenezer Morse (1718–1802)
 d. Boylston, Mass.; HC 1737
John Newman (1715/6–1763)
 d. Edgartown, Mass.; HC 1740
Samuel Palmer (1707–1775)
 d. Falmouth, Mass.; HC 1727
Jonathan Parsons (1705–1770)
 d. Newburyport, Mass.; YC 1729
Joseph Pynchon (1704/5–1765)
 d. Boston, Mass.; HC 1726
Mathew Rockwell (1707/8–1782)
 d. East Windsor, Conn.; YC 1728
John Shaw (1708–1791)
 d. Bridgewater, Mass.; HC 1729
John Smith (1702–1771)
 d. White Plains, NY; YC 1727
William Throop (1720–1756)
 d. Southold, Long Island; YC 1743
Samuel Webster (1718–1796)
 d. Amesbury, Mass.; HC 1737
John Wilson (1721–1776)
 d. Hopkinton, Mass.; HC 1741
Ebenezer Winchester (1725–1756)
 d. Hingham, Mass.; HC 1744

Group 7: 1751–1770 (N=22)

James Baker (1739–1825)
  d. Dorchester, Mass.; HC 1760
Jonathan Bird (1746/7–1813)
  d. Hebron, Conn.; YC 1768
Nathaniel Bond (1746–1777)
  d. Newton, Penn.; HC 1766
Joshua Brackett (1733–1802)
  d. Portsmouth, N.H.; HC 1742
Samuel Cary (1734–1784)
  d. Lyme, Conn.; YC 1755
Jonathan Crane (1738–1813)
  d. Bridgewater, Mass.; HC 1762
Mannaseh Cutler (1742–1823)
  d. Hamilton, Mass.; YC 1765
Samuel Eells (1744/5–1808)
  d. North Branford, Conn.; YC
  1765
Joshua Elderkin (1720–1801)
  d. Canterbury, Conn.; YC 1748
Eli Forbes (1726–1804)
  d. Gloucester, Mass.; HC 1751
Justus Forward (1730–1814)
  d. Belchertown, Mass.; HC 1754
Nathaniel Hooker (1737–1770)
  d. West Hartford, Conn.; YC
  1755

Abner Johnson (1738–1817)
  d. Waterbury, Conn.; YC 1759
Eneas Munson (1734–1826)
  d. New Haven, Conn.; YC 1753
Joseph Perry (1731–1783)
  d. South Windsor, Conn.; HC
  1752
Asaph Rice (1733–1816)
  d. Westminster, Mass.(?); HC
  1752
David Rose (1736–1799)
  d. Southhaven, Conn.; YC 1760
Samuel Seabury (1729–1796)
  d. New London, Conn.; YC
  1748
Solomon Sprague (1730–1794)
  d. Exeter, R.I.
Antipas Steward (1733–1808)
  d. Belchertown, Mass.; HC 1760
Joseph Thaxter (1742–1827)
  d. Edgartown, Mass.; HC 1768
Eleazer Wales (1732–1794)
  d. Chester, Mass.; YC 1753

Removed to England

John Allin (1623–1682)
  d. unknown; HC 1643
Isaac Chauncy (1632–1711/12)
  d. London; HC 1661
Rowland Cotton (1674–1753)
  d. Billaport, England; HC 1696
Nathaniel Eaton (1609–1674)
  d. Bideford, Devon, England;
  CU 1629

Giles Firmin (1614–1697)
  d. England
Thomas Larkham (1602–1669)
  d. Tavistock, England; CU 1621
Samuel Lee (1625–1691)
  d. St. Malo, French prison; OU
  1648

Appendix 2

Number of Moves Made by Ministers

(N=126) Group	Not Available	No Moves	One Move	Two Moves	Three or More Moves
1* (1630–1650)	0.00%	0.00%	6.25%	31.25%	62.50%
2 (1651–1670)	0.00	0.00	16.67	50.00	33.33
3 (1671–1690)	18.18	9.09	18.18	9.09	45.45
4 (1691–1710)	6.67	6.67	33.33	20.00	33.33
5 (1711–1730)	4.55	4.55	31.82	4.55	54.53
6 (1731–1750)	0.00	3.45	31.03	27.59	37.93
7 (1751–1770)	4.76	4.76	19.05	19.05	52.38

*The high mobility of immigrant divines reflects their removal to New England from the mother country. During the early years of settlement, many ministers resettled with their entire communities in more desirable areas. Thus the high mobility figures for Group 1 do not indicate job instability.

Notes

Abbreviations

AAS   American Antiquarian Society, Worcester, Massachusetts
HC   Harvard College, Cambridge, Massachusetts
NEHGR *New England Historical and Genealogical Register*
NEHGS New England Historical and Genealogical Society, Boston
          Massachusetts
YC   Yale College, New Haven, Connecticut

Introduction

1. Cotton Mather, *Magnalia Christi Americana; or the Ecclesiastical History of New England* (London: Thomas Parkhurst, 1702), 1:439. Henry M. Parrish claims that the clergy assumed a "lion's share of early medical practice in the colonies where there was a shortage of trained physicians." Parrish, "Contributions of the Clergy to Early American Medicine," *Journal of the Bowman Gray School of Medicine* 14 (1956):55–73. James H. Cassedy claims that the angelical conjunction was "an activity that filled an essential need in society during a time trained physicians were few and far between." "Church Record-Keeping and Public Health in Early New England," in Cassedy, *Medicine in Colonial Massachusetts*, ed. Philip Cash, Eric H. Christianson, and J. Worth Estes, 249–62 (Boston: Colonial Society of Massachusetts, 1980). For similar interpretations, see Eric H. Christianson, "The Medical Practitioners of Massachusetts, 1630–1800: Patterns of Change and Continuity," in Cash, Christianson, and Estes, *Medicine in Colonial Massachusetts*, 51; Richard D. Brown, "The Healing Arts in Colonial and Revolutionary Massachusetts: The Context for Scientific Medicine," in Cash, Christianson, and Estes, *Medicine in Colonial Massachusetts*, 38–39; and Henry R. Viets, *A Brief History of Medicine in Massachusetts* (Boston: Houghton Mifflin, 1930), 1, 7.

2. On the high cost of professional medical care and the widespread

poverty in 17th-century England, see Doreen Evenden Nagy, *Popular Medicine in Seventeenth-Century England* (Bowling Green, Ohio: Bowling Green Univ. Press, 1988). "Letters of Samuel Lee and Samuel Sewall Relating to New England and the Indians," *Publications* of the Colonial Society of Massachusetts 14 (1912):146–47; "Letter from Giles Firmin to Governor John Winthrop," *Collections* of the Massachusetts Historical Society, 4th series (1865), 273–76; Christianson, "Medical Practitioners," 54; Charles Webster and Margaret Pelling, "Medical Practitioners," in *Health, Medicine and Mortality in the Sixteenth Century*, ed. Charles Webster (Cambridge, England: Cambridge Univ. Press, 1979), 191–92.

3. Julius H. Tuttle, "The Libraries of the Mathers," *Proceedings* of the AAS 20 (1910):270; George Selement, *Keepers of the Vineyard: The Puritan Ministry and Collective Culture in Colonial New England* (Lanham, Mass.: University Press of America, 1984), 28. On the uniformity of the 17th-century colonies in Connecticut and Massachusetts, see the extraordinary work of Perry Miller, *The New England Mind: The Seventeenth Century* (Cambridge, Mass.: Belknap Press of Harvard Univ. Press, 1953), 398, and David D. Hall, *Worlds of Wonder, Days of Judgment: Popular Religious Belief in Early New England* (New York: Knopf, 1989), 6–10.

4. John Brown, *Divine Help Implored Under the Loss of Godly and Faithful Men. A Funeral Sermon for the Reverend Mr. Thomas Symmes,* (Boston: T. Fleet, 1726), 34, 37.

5. Keith Thomas, *Religion and the Decline of Magic* (New York: Scribner's, 1971), 275, 250. Michael MacDonald, *Mystical Bedlam: Madness, Anxiety and Healing in Seventeenth-Century England* (Cambridge, England: Cambridge Univ. Press, 1981), 32. On the contentiousness of the churches in colonial New England, see David D. Hall, *The Faithful Shepherd: A History of the New England Ministry in the Seventeenth Century* (Chapel Hill: Univ. of North Carolina Press, 1972), 186–194.

Chapter 1

1. Samuel Willard, *A Compleat Body of Divinity* (New York: Johnson Reprint Corp., 1969), 224–25. The passage from Willard is based on Gen. 3:16–19.

2. Samuel Danforth, *A Brief Recognition of New-Englands Errand into the Wilderness* (Cambridge, Mass., 1671), 64–65, quoted in Sacvan Bercovitch, *The American Jeremiad* (Madison: Univ. of Wisconsin Press, 1978), 16. On the relationship between religion and healing in the western Christian traditions, see the essays in Martin E. Marty and Kenneth L. Vaux, eds., *Health/*

Medicine and the Faith Traditions (Philadelphia: Fortress Press, 1982); Ronald L. Numbers and Darrel W. Amundsen, eds., *Caring and Curing: Health and Medicine in the Western Religious Traditions* (New York: Macmillan, 1986); and W.J. Sheils, ed., *The Church and Healing* (Oxford, England: Basil Blackwell, 1982).

3. For an analysis of the Puritans' emphasis on the parallels between the Israelites' exile and the Puritan "mission" in New England, see Bercovitch, *American Jeremiad*, 3–33. Also see Kenneth B. Murdock, *Literature and Theology in Colonial New England* (Cambridge, Mass.: Harvard Univ. Press, 1949), 122–24, and Perry Miller's excellent section in *New England Mind: 17th Century*, 463–91. The first two quotes are from Perry Miller, *New England Mind: 17th Century*, 475, 481. On the centrality of the covenant in early New England, see Perry Miller, *New England Mind: 17th Century* chs. 13, 14, and 15. The quote from Winthrop is from his *A Model of Christian Charity* (1630), quoted in Perry Miller, *New England Mind: 17th Century*, 477. Thomas Hooker's quote is also from Perry Miller, *New England Mind: 17th Century*, 482.

4. John Cotton, *Gods Mercie Mixed with his Justice: or His Peoples Deliverance in Time of Danger Laid Open in Severall Sermons*, (London, 1641), p. 118. On lay preoccupation with the relationship between sickness and sin, see Kenneth P. Minkema, "The East Windsor Conversion Relations, 1700–1725," *Bulletin* of the Connecticut Historical Society 51 (1986):27, 33, 35, 43, 47, 50, 54. Also see Patricia Caldwell, *The Puritan Conversion Narrative: The Beginnings of American Expression* (Cambridge, England: Cambridge Univ. Press, 1983). On the clergy's duty to record and interpret remarkable providences, see Perry Miller and Thomas H. Johnson, *The Puritans: A Sourcebook of Their Writings*, rev. ed. (New York: Harper and Row, 1963), 2:735.

5. Darrel W. Amundsen, "The Medieval Catholic Tradition," in Numbers and Amundsen, *Caring and Curing*, 78.

6. Darrel W. Amundsen and Gary Ferngren, "Medicine and Religion: Early Christianity Through the Middle Ages," in Marty and Vaux, *Health/Medicine*, 125.

7. Amundsen, "Medieval Catholic Tradition," 76; Richard Palmer, "The Church, Leprosy and Plague in Medieval and Early Modern Europe," in Sheils, *Church and Healing*, 83.

8. The causal connection established between sickness and sin in *The Book of Common Prayer* was not revised until 1892. The quote is from "The Great Litany," originally published in 1544 and included in the prayer book, as quoted in John E. Booty, "The Anglican Tradition," in Numbers and Amundsen, *Caring and Curing*, 248, 243, 249.

9. William Perkins, *A Salve for A Sicke Man* (London, 1596), 25, 32.

10. Booty, "Anglican Tradition," 243; Stanley W. Jackson, "Robert Burton and Psychological Healing," *Journal of the History of Medicine and Allied*

Sciences 44 (1989):160–78. Like Burton, Baxter believed that melancholia should be treated through a combination of physical and proper spiritual healing. He suggested that "medicinal remedies and theological use" should not be administered "together by the same hand; but, in this case of perfect complication of the maladies of mind and body, I think it not unfit, if I do it not unskilfully." While Baxter was greatly revered by Protestants on both sides of the Atlantic, he was a moderate Presbyterian and a critic of New England's Congregational system of church polity. Richard Baxter, "The Cure of Melancholy and Overmuch Sorrow by Faith and Physic," in Baxter, *Puritan Sermons 1659–1689, Being the Morning Exercises at Cripplegate, St. Giles in the Fields, and In Southwark by Seventy-Five Ministers of the Gospel in or Near London*, 6 vols. (Wheaton, Ill.: Richard Owen Roberts, 1981), 3:263; 3:266–67; 3:285. For a biography of Baxter, see Frederick J. Powicke, *A Life of the Reverend Richard Baxter, 1615–1691* (London, 1924).

11. Perry Miller, *The New England Mind: From Colony to Providence* (Cambridge, Mass.: Belknap Press of Harvard Univ. Press, 1953), 54–58.

12. Journal entry for 16 Jan. 1712/13, in Samuel E. Morison, "The Commonplace Book of Joseph Green," *Publications* of the Colonial Society of Massachusetts 34 (1937–42):253; Amundsen, "Medieval Catholic Tradition," 97; Cotton Mather, *The Angel of Bethesda*, ed. Gordon H. Jones (Worcester, Mass.: AAS, 1972), 6.

13. Edmund S. Morgan, "The Diary of the Rev. Michael Wigglesworth," *Publications* of the Colonial Society of Massachusetts 35 (1946):376.

14. Ibid., 316, 401. For a detailed analysis of the Puritan's social covenant theory, see Miller, *New England Mind: 17th Century*, 398–431.

15. "Rev. John Eliot's Records of the First Church in Roxbury, Mass.," NEHGR 33 (1879):236–38.

16. John Duffy, *The Healers: The Rise of the Medical Establishment* (New York: McGraw-Hill, 1976), 8–15.

17. "Rev. John Eliot's Records," 236–38. W. Deloss Love, Jr., *The Fast and Thanksgiving Days of New England* (Boston: Houghton Mifflin, 1895), 41–51. A.K. Teele, ed., *The History of Milton, Massachusetts, 1640–1887* (Milton, Mass., 1887), 652.

18. Love, *Fast and Thanksgiving Days*, 183–87. Also see Miller, *New England Mind: Colony to Province*, 20, 346; and John B. Blake, "The Inoculation Controversy in Boston, 1721–22," in *Sickness and Health in America*, ed. Judith E. Leavitt and Ronald L. Numbers (Madison: Univ. of Wisconsin Press, 1978), 231. Ernest Caulfield, "Some Common Diseases of Colonial Children," *Publications* of the Colonial Society of Massachusetts 35 (1942–46):13; Daniel Boorstin, *The Americans: The Colonial Experience* (New York: Vintage, 1958), 219–20. For a more detailed account, see John Duffy, *Epidemics in Colonial America* (Baton Rouge: Louisiana State Univ. Press, 1953).

19. James R. Henretta, "The Morphology of New England Society in the Colonial Period," *Journal of Interdisciplinary History* 2 (1972):385, 391. Timothy H. Breen and Stephen Foster, "The Puritans' Greatest Achievement: A Study of Social Cohesion in Seventeenth Century Massachusetts," *Journal of American History* 60 (1973):9. Also see David Zuckerman, *Peaceable Kingdoms: New England Towns in the Eighteenth Century* (New York: Knopf, 1970).

20. David E. Stannard, *The Puritan Way of Death: A Study of Religion, Culture and Social Change* (Oxford, England: Oxford Univ. Press, 1977), 57; Gordon E. Geddes, *Welcome Joy: Death in Puritan New England* (Ann Arbor, Mich.: UMI Research Press, 1981), 38–39.

21. Darrett B. Rutman and Anita Rutman, "Of Agues and Fever: Malaria in the Early Chesapeake," *William and Mary Quarterly*, 3d ser., 33 (1976):31–60. On attitudes towards death in early New England, see Maris A. Vinovskis, "Angels' Heads and Weeping Willows: Death in Early America," in *Studies in American Historical Demography: Essays in the History of the Family* (Worcester, Mass.: AAS, 1976), 288–301. On the New England colonists' perceptions of some diseases as purely natural phenomena, see John Demos, *Entertaining Satan: Witchcraft and the Culture of Early New England* (New York: Oxford Univ. Press, 1982), 168. Bercovitch, *American Jeremiad*, 8–9.

22. Miller and Johnson, *The Puritans*, 2:614.

23. Bercovitch, *American Jeremiad*, xi–30. The "Citty upon a Hill" reference is from John Winthrop's lay-sermon, "A Modell of Christian Charity." It is reprinted in Miller and Johnson, *The Puritans*, 1:195–99.

24. Rev. Samuel Danforth, Roxbury Church Records," NEHGR 34 (1880): 86; F.J. Powicke, ed., "Some Unpublished Correspondence Between the Reverend Richard Baxter and the Reverend John Eliot, 1656–1682," *Bulletin of the John Rylands Library* 15 (1931):154. Geddes, *Welcome Joy*, 42; Amundsen and Ferngren, "Early Christianity," 94–95; Cotton Mather, *Magnalia*, 2:23.

25. Raymond P. Stearns, ed., "The Correspondence of John Woodbridge, Jr., and Richard Baxter," *New England Quarterly* 10 (1937):572; Mather, *Angel of Bethesda*, 93–94; Richard L. Bushman, *From Puritan to Yankee: Character and the Social Order in Connecticut, 1690–1765* (Cambridge, Mass.: Harvard Univ. Press, 1967; rptd. 1980), 267.

26. Hall, *Worlds of Wonder*, 196–212, 226–29. The conversion relations of Ann Fitch and Hannah Bancroft Samuel may be found in Minkema, "East Windsor Conversions," 33, 27. The quote on death is from Ebenezer Gay, *The Sovereignty of God, in determining Man's Days, or the Time & Manner of his Death* (Hartford, Conn., 1767), 9.

27. Perkins, *A Salve*, 25. Ronald C. Sawyer, "Patients, Healers and Disease in the Southeast Midlands, 1597–1634" (Ph.D. diss., Univ. of Wisconsin, Madison, 1986), 242–43; a revised version of this work is forthcoming from Cambridge Univ. Press.

28. Hall, *Worlds of Wonder*, 5–6. On literacy in New England, see Kenneth Lockridge, *Literacy in Colonial New England: An Enquiry into the Social Context of Literacy in the Early Modern West* (New York: Norton, 1974), and David D. Hall, "The Uses of Literacy," in Hall, *Worlds of Wonder*, 21–70.

The most recent effort to characterize a "collective mentality" for early New England is David Hall's penetrating *Worlds of Wonder*. Also see Hall, "The World of Print and Collective Mentality in Seventeenth-Century New England," in *New Directions in American Intellectual History*, ed. John Higham and Paul Conkin (Baltimore, Md.: Johns Hopkins Univ. Press, 1979), 156–80. Perry Miller, Sacvan Bercovitch, and Alan Heimert have also argued that the laity shared the priorities of the educated elite. See Perry Miller, "The Preparation for Salvation," in *Nature's Nation* (Cambridge, Mass.: Belknap, Press of Harvard Univ. Press, 1967), 50–77; and Sacvan Bercovitch, *The American Puritan Imagination: Essays in Revaluation* (Cambridge, Mass.: Harvard Univ. Press, 1974), and *American Jeremiad*.

Darrett B. Rutman and Paul Lucas have argued the opposite case, that two separate cultures existed in New England, one of the clergy and the other of the laity they served. See Rutman's *Winthrop's Boston: A Portrait of a Puritan Town, 1630–1649* (Chapel Hill: Univ. of North Carolina Press, 1965) and Paul Lucas, *Valley of Discord* (Hanover, N.H.: Univ. Presses of New England, 1976).

29. Ronald Numbers and Darrel Amundsen, "The Early Christian Tradition," in Numbers and Amundsen, *Caring and Curing*, 46; Increase Mather, *Memorable Providences* (London: Reeves and Turner, 1890), 119. On Satan's powers, see Paul H. Kocher, *Science and Religion in Elizabethan England* (San Marino, Calif.: Huntington Library, 1953), 121–27; Richard Baxter, *Puritan Sermons*, 262, 285.

30. On the widespread belief in demons and witches during the 17th century, see Keith Thomas, *Religion and the Decline of Magic*, chs. 14–18. Cotton Mather, *Remarkable Providences, Relating to Witchcrafts and Possessions* (Boston, 1689), 63; and Cotton Mather, "A Discourse on Witchcraft," in *Remarkable Providences*, 6. [Heinrich Kramer and Jakob Sprenger], *Malleus Maleficarum*, trans. Rev. Montague Summers (rpt. ed., New York: Benjamin Blom, 1970), 115. Echoing biblical precedent and English law, the Massachusetts Body of Liberties of 1641 stated, "If any man or woman be a witch (that is hath or consulteth with a familiar spirit) they shall be put to death." William H. Whitmore, ed., *The Colonial Laws of Massachusetts, Reprinted from the Edition of 1660, with the Supplements to 1672. Containing also the Body of Liberties of 1641* (Boston: City Council, 1889), 55. For English witchcraft laws, see Wallace Notestein, *A History of Witchcraft in England from 1558 to 1718* (rpt. ed., New York: Russell and Russell, 1965), 12. Deut. 18:10–12 states: "There must never be any one among you . . . who practices divination, who is a sooth-

sayer, auger, or sorcerer, who uses charms, consults ghosts or spirits, or calls up the dead." Lev. 20:27 reads, "Any man or woman who is a necromancer or magician must be put to death by stoning." The witchcraft quotes are from Sarah Loring Bailey, *Historical Sketches of Andover, Massachusetts* (Cambridge, Mass., 1880), 203; W. Elliot Woodward, *Records of Salem Witchcraft Copied from the Original Documents*, 2 vols. (Roxbury, Mass.: Privately printed, 1864; rpt. ed., New York: Da Capo Press, 1969), 2:9; and 1:95–96, as quoted in Paul Boyer and Stephen Nissenbaum, *Salem Possessed: The Social Origins of Witchcraft* (Cambridge, Mass.: Harvard Univ. Press, 1974), 14–15. For a brief overview of the various theories explaining the outbreak of witchcraft accusations in Salem, see Chadwick Hansen, "Andover Witchcraft and the Causes of the Salem Witchcraft Trials," in *The Occult in America*, ed. Howard Kerr and Charles L. Crow (Urbana: Univ. of Illinois Press, 1983), 38–55. For a more generic overview of witchcraft historiography, see David D. Hall, "Witchcraft and the Limits of Interpretation," *New England Quarterly* 58 (1985):253–81. For accounts of illness related to witchcraft in New England, see Demos, *Entertaining Satan*, 39–40, 44, 46, 81–84, 139–40, 143, 145, 166–70, 193–94, 213–20, 290, 293, 306, 319, 361. On cases of illness connected to witchcraft in Essex, England, see ch. 13 in Alan Macfarlane, *Witchcraft in Tudor and Stuart England* (New York: Harper and Row, 1970), 178–210. It is interesting to note that Essex had a higher incidence of witchcraft accusations than the rest of England, and "Essex supplied a disproportionately large complement of settlers for the new colonies across the sea" (p. 12).

31. [Kramer and Sprenger], *Malleus Maleficarum*, 87; Increase Mather, *Remarkable Providences*, 119–22. The quote by Willis is from his book *Of Convulsive Diseases*, ch. 2, p. 11, reprinted in *Dr. Willis' Practice of Physick, Being the Whole Works of That . . . Physician* (London, 1684), as quoted in Owsei Temkin, *The Falling Sickness: A History of Epilepsy from the Greeks to the Beginning of Modern Neurology* (Baltimore, Md.: Johns Hopkins Univ. Press, 1971). The interpretation of epilepsy as a natural disease is rooted in the Hippocratic Corpus, with which Mather claimed familiarity. A number of physicians in the 16th and 17th centuries also characterized epilepsy as a natural disease, and they felt it was their responsibility to distinguish it from demonic possession. See Temkin, *Falling Sickness*, 141–44. Amundsen and Ferngren, "Medicine and Religion: From Pre-Christian Antiquity," 97.

32. [Kramer and Sprenger], *Malleus Maleficarum*, 87; Macfarlane, *Witchcraft in England*, 143–48.

33. Demos, *Entertaining Satan*, 99, 103, 106, 111, 130; his account of the Willard case is 99–130. Willard's account is fully reprinted in Samuel A. Green, *Groton in Witchcraft Times* (Groton, Mass.: J. Wilson & Sons, 1883), 7–21.

34. Demos, *Entertaining Satan*, 116.

35. John Hale, *A modest enquiry into the nature of witchcraft* (Boston, 1702), 26; Demos, *Entertaining Satan*, 363, 182–84.

36. Cotton Mather, *Remarkable Providences*, 3, 5–6, 31–32, 47–48.

37. Thomas, *Religion and the Decline*, 127–28. On Practical Divinity, see Michael MacDonald, "Religion, Social Change, and Psychological Healing in England, 1600–1800," in Sheils, *Church and Healing*, 101–126. Miller and Johnson, *The Puritans*, 2:735; Demos, *Entertaining Satan*, 98–99.

38. On English countermagic, see Thomas, *Religion and the Decline*, 39, 49, 229, 249, 494, 497, 543–44, 634–35, 649. Cotton Mather, *Remarkable Providences*, 5. Demos, *Entertaining Satan*, 182–84; and, on New England countermagic, 8, 138–39, 147, 193, 199, 217, 280, 331, 390–91.

39. Clive Holmes, "Popular Culture? Witches, Magistrates, and Divines in Early Modern England," in *Understanding Popular Culture: Europe from the Middle Ages to the Nineteenth Century*, ed. Steven Kaplan (Berlin: Mouton, 1984), 104, 85–111. On the practices of the English cunning folk, see Thomas, *Religion and the Decline*, chs. 7 and 8, and Macfarlane, *Witchcraft in England*, ch. 8.

40. Cotton Mather, *Angel of Bethesda*, 122, 294–97.

41. Sawyer, "Patients, Healers and Disease," 236–41.

42. John Langdon Sibley, *Biographical Sketches of the Graduates of Harvard University*, 17 vols. (Cambridge, Mass.: Charles William Sever, 1873–1975), 1:386. The Aramaic expression "Ephphatha" may have been used to enhance the sense of supernatural power in this act of healing. For further explanation, see *Interpreter's Dictionary of the Bible*, 4 vols. (New York: Abingdon Press, 1962), 1:119. While the Protestant Reformation stripped the priest of most of his "magical" functions (including exorcism, formulae of benediction and consecrations, and celibacy), the association between magical healing and the priesthood only gradually faded in early modern England. According to Keith Thomas, the "sorceror-parson" was "not extinguished by the Reformation, for as late as the 19th century there were some parish clergy who enjoyed a magical reputation among their parishioners." See Thomas, *Religion and the Decline*, 277, 535–48. The quote on the Apostles is from Ebenezer Pemberton, *A Sermon Preached . . . To which is added, A brief DISCOURSE upon the divine Appointment of the Gospel Ministry* (Boston: J. Draper, 1738), 23, 25.

43. Sibley, *Harvard Graduates*, 4:334–45; George Herbert, *The Countrey Parson and Selected Poems*, ed. Hugh Martin (London: SCM Press, 1956); Thomas, *Religion and the Decline*, 275–77.

44. Ebenezer Parkman, *The Diary of Ebenezer Parkman, 1703–1782*, ed. Francis G. Walett (Worcester, Mass.: American Antiquarian Society, 1974), 165. See the collection of essays in Wayland D. Hand, ed., *American Folk*

Medicine (Berkeley: Univ. of California Press, 1976), for the survival of magical concepts in American folk healing.

45. Thomas Symmes, manuscript notebook, 1696–1774, AAS. On the elusiveness of popular culture in Europe, as well as the profound degree of fluidity and interchange between so-called popular and elite concepts, see David D. Hall's "Introduction" to Kaplan, *Understanding Popular Culture*, 5–18.

Chapter 2

1. Amundsen and Ferngren, "Early Christianity," 93–131. Also see Amundsen, "Medieval Catholic Tradition," 65–107.

2. Amundsen and Ferngren, "Early Christianity," 107–115. Darrel Amundsen points out that it is a mistake to view these early Christian facilities for caring for the sick as hospitals in the modern sense of the word. Rather, these structures, usually attached to a cathedral or other church, provided refuge to poor, weary travelers in need of food, shelter, and rudimentary medical care. During the later Middle Ages and the Renaissance, such institutions developed into facilities which provided medical care on a more organized basis. See Amundsen, "Medieval Catholic Tradition," 83, and Amundsen and Ferngren, "Early Christianity," 107–115. Henry Sigerist, *Civilization and Disease* (Ithaca, N.Y.: Cornell Univ. Press, 1943), 69–70; Kocher, *Science and Religion*, 226; Whitney R.D. Jones, *William Turner: Tudor Naturalist, Physician and Divine* (London: Routledge, 1988), 101.

3. Huling E. Ussery, *Chaucer's Physician: Medicine and Literature in Fourteenth Century England* (New Orleans: Tulane Studies in English, no. 19, 1971), 28–31. *Diary of the Rev. John Ward, A.M., Vicar of Stratford-upon-Avon, Extending From 1648–1679*, ed. Charles Severn, (London: Henry Colburn, 1838), 117.

4. Robert S. Gottfried, "English Medical Practitioners, 1340–1530," *Bulletin of the History of Medicine* 58 (1984):181, 164–82. On the role of the English clergy in medieval medical practice, see Charles Talbot, *Medicine in Medieval England* (London: Oldbourne, 1967), 198–211; E.A. Hammond and Charles Talbot, *The Medical Practitioners in Medieval England* (London: Wellcome Historical Medical Library, 1965); Stanley Rubin, *Medieval English Medicine* (London: David and Charles, 1974), 70–96; Edward J. Kealey, *Medieval Medicus: A Social History of Anglo-Norman Medicine* (Baltimore, Md.: Johns Hopkins Univ. Press, 1981); and Rosamond J. Mitchell, *John Free: From Bristol to Rome in the Fifteenth Century* (London: Longman, Green, 1955), 16–17. Pelling and Webster, "Medical Practitioners," 199.

5. On the high cost of secular medical care and the widespread poverty

of 17th-century England, see Nagy, *Popular Medicine in Seventeenth-Century England*. John T. McNeil, *A History of the Cure of Souls* (New York: Harper and Row, 1951), vii–viii, 40, 95; Herbert, *The Countrey Parson*, 45–62. John Cotton, *A Briefe Exposition upon Ecclesiastes* (London, 1654), as quoted in Theodore Hornberger, "Puritanism and Science: The Relationship Revealed in the Writings of John Cotton," *New England Quarterly* 10 (1937):513–14.

6. Gabriel Plattes, *Macaria* (London, 1641), as quoted in Charles Webster, *The Great Instauration: Science, Medicine and Reform, 1626–1660* (London: Duckworth, 1975), 259. This book is an extremely important study of the connections between Puritanism and the advancement of science in early modern England. Webster's work has been attacked by historians who have stressed the Anglican origins of modern science. For example, see James R. Jacob and Margaret C. Jacob, "The Anglican Origins of Modern Science: The Metaphysical Foundations of the Whig Constitution," *ISIS* 71 (1980):251–67.

7. Cotton Mather, *Magnalia*, 2:250, 1:494. William Durrant Cooper, "Notices of the Last Great Plague, 1665–6, From the Letters of John Allin to Philip Fryth and Samuel Jeake," *Archaeologica* 37 (1857):10–11.

8. Miller, *New England Mind: Colony to Province*, 353. William Willis, *Journals of the Rev. Thomas Smith and the Rev. Samuel Deane* (Portland, Me.: Joseph J. Bailey, 1849), 172; *The Letters of John Davenport, Puritan Divine* (New Haven, Conn.: Published for the First Church of Christ in New Haven by Yale Univ. Press, 1937), 183. Parkman Family Papers, c. 1772, AAS; Francis G. Walett, *The Diary of Ebenezer Parkman, 1703–1755* (Worcester, Mass.: AAS, 1974), 254.

9. Thomas Thacher, *A Brief Rule*, ed. Harry R. Viets (Baltimore, Md.: Johns Hopkins Univ. Press, 1937), xiii–liv.

10. Ronald Numbers and Ronald Sawyer, "Medicine and Christianity in the Modern World," in Marty and Vaux, *Health/Medicine*, 141; Selement, *Keepers of the Vineyard*, 28–29.

11. "The Glorious Progresse of the Gospel Against the Indians of New England," *Collections* of the Massachusetts Historical Society, 3rd ser., 4 (1834):77.

12. Peter Thacher's diary entry is from 17 Jan. 1682, in Teele, *History of Milton, Mass.*, 647.

13. Cotton Mather, "The Life of Thomas Thacher," in *Magnalia*, bk. 3, ch. 26, p. 151; Hugh Adams, Autobiographical Narratives in the Belknap Manuscripts, ms. dated 7 Dec. 1724, p. 23, Massachusetts Historical Society; Sibley, *Harvard Graduates*, 4:325.

14. Darrel W. Amundsen, "Medieval Canon Law on Medical and Surgical Practice by the Clergy," *Bulletin of the History of Medicine* 52 (1978):28–30. For a comparison of the economic levels of the professions in early modern England, see Rosemary O'Day, *The English Clergy: The Emergence and Consolidation of a Profession, 1558–1642* (Leicester: Leicester Univ. Press, 1979), 176–77. Thomas, *Religion and the Decline of Magic*, 275.

15. Webster and Pelling, "Medical Practitioners," 199–200; Thomas, *Religion and the Decline of Magic*, 275; O'Day, *English Clergy*, 176–77.

16. O'Day, *English Clergy*, 172–89, 194–207.

17. Robert Burton, *The Anatomy of Melancholy*, i, 36, as quoted in Thomas, *Religion and the Decline*, 250, 275. MacDonald, *Mystical Bedlam*, 32. On clerical salaries, see Hall, *Faithful Shepherd*, 66–67.

18. Duffy, *The Healers*, 18; Webster and Pelling, "Medical Practitioners," 188.

19. Vanessa S. Doe, ed., *The Diary of James Clegg of Chapel en le Frith, 1708–1755*, pts. 1 and 2, 3 vols. (Derbyshire, England: Derbyshire Record Society, 1978), 1:xxxiv–xxxv. A.G. Matthews, *Calamy Revised: Being a Revision of Edmund Calamy's Account of the Ministers and Others Ejected and Silenced, 1660–1662* (Oxford, England: Clarendon Press, 1934), xvi.

20. Matthews, *Calamy Revised*, lvii–lviii, 71, 409.

21. Probate 4, Docket #1820, Will P.C.C., St. Walbury's Parish, Bristol, 30 Oct. 1675. Viets, *Brief History of Medicine in Massachusetts*, 36–43; John Ward Dean, "A Brief Memoir of the Rev. Giles Firmin, One of the Ejected Ministers of 1662," NEHGR (1866), offprint, 14–15; Matthews, *Calamy Revised*, 197.

22. C. Helen Brock, "The Influence of Europe on Colonial Massachusetts Medicine," in Cash, Christianson, and Estes, *Medicine in Colonial Massachusetts*, 104; Wilson Waters, *The History of Chelmsford, Massachusetts* (Lowell, Mass.: 1917), 17, as quoted in Ola E. Winslow, *A Destroying Angel: The Conquest of Smallpox in Colonial Boston* (Boston: Houghton Mifflin, 1974), 12; Robert G. Pope, "The Notebook of the Rev. John Fiske, 1644–1675," *Publications* of the Colonial Society of Massachusetts 47 (1974):ix–x. Thomas Gage, *The History of Rowley, Anciently Including Bradford, Boxford, and Georgetown . . .* (Boston: Ferdinand and Andrews, 1840), 39; Cotton Mather, *Magnalia*, 1:40. Ralph Partridge (1579–1658) also came to New England with two professions; see William Sprague, *Annals of the American Pulpit*, 9 vols. (New York: R. Carter and Bros., 1859–[73]), 1:90. Herbert, *The Countrey Parson*, 70.

23. Hall, *Faithful Shepherd*, 186 and 194. Pope, *Notebook of John Fiske*, ix–xiv and xxxviii.

24. Edmund S. Morgan, *Visible Saints: The History of a Puritan Idea*, 1963; (rptd. Ithaca, N.Y.: Cornell Univ. Press, 1975), 130–39.

25. Bushman, *Puritan to Yankee*, 148–50; Hall, *Faithful Shepherd*, 194.

26. Doe, *Diary of James Clegg*, 1:xlii, 248.

27. Sibley, *Harvard Graduates*, 1:166–70.

28. Hall, *Faithful Shepherd*, 146–49; William Chauncy Fowler, *Memorials of the Chauncys, Including President Chauncy, His Ancestors, And Descendants*, 2d ed. (Boston, 1858; rpt. ed. Owensboro, TX: McDowell, 1981), 16–26.

29. Hall, *Faithful Shepherd*, 146–49.

30. Ibid., 190–94, 266.

31. Ibid., 187; Breen and Foster, "Puritans' Greatest Achievement," 20.

32. Edwin J. Perkins, *The Economy of Colonial America* (New York: Columbia Univ. Press, 1980), 1. For a study of those ejected under the Act of Uniformity in England, see Matthews, *Calamy Revised*.

33. For more on Chauncy's medical career, see R.W. Innes-Smith, *English-Speaking Students of Medicine at the University of Leyden* (Edinburgh: Oliver and Boyd, 1931), 44.

34. Sibley, *Harvard Graduates*, 2:270. Abner Johnson (YC 1759) of Waterbury, Conn., also had to abandon the ministry because of poor health. Then, with the aid of his wife, an accomplished herbalist, he became a druggist. See Franklin B. Dexter, *Biographical Sketches of the Graduates of Yale College: With Annals of College History*, 6 vols. (New York: Holt, 1885–1912), 2:599–600. Many ministers gave up their careers in divinity claiming poor health, but, as Michael Wigglesworth's testimonial indicates, the reasons for a minister's relinquishing the pulpit often were much more complex than those that he admitted publicly. Gershom Bulkeley (HC 1651), Wigglesworth's classmate at Harvard, claimed that he left the ministry because of the weakness of his voice. Yet an examination of data on his earlier pastorates indicates that he was often at odds with his parishioners over such issues as his opposition to the half-way convenant. In addition, he was a remarkably litigious individual, constantly bringing people to court over matters such as their failure to pay his medical bills. Such litigiousness probably did little to advance his clerical career. See Sibley, *Harvard Graduates*, 2:389–402. Morgan, "Diary of Michael Wigglesworth," 314. Michael Wigglesworth, "Some Grounds and Reasons for Laying Down My Office Related," manuscript, NEHGS.

35. Bushman, *Puritan to Yankee*, 147–63; Sibley, *Harvard Graduates*, 6:406; Hugh Adams, Manuscript Narrative, 28–29, quoted in Sibley, *Harvard Graduates*, 4:325; Sibley, *Harvard Graduates*, 4:334–35; Eric Christianson, "The Medical Practitioners of Massachusetts," 56–61. Christianson found that, while doctors were less stable geographically than the general population, those healers without apprenticeship or college training moved significantly more often than their trained counterparts, indicating repeated failure to secure a successful practice. Hugh Adams, Autobiographical Narratives, 23.

36. Sibley, *Harvard Graduates*, 4:290–93.

37. Bruce Tucker, "The Reinterpretation of Puritan History," *New England Quarterly* 54 (1981):481. Morgan, *Visible Saints*, 150–52; Bushman, *Puritan to Yankee*, 147–63.

38. Dexter, *Yale Graduates*, 1:151–54. Stephen Wickes, *The History of Medicine in New Jersey* (Newark, N.J.: M.R. Dennis and Co., 1879), 167–68; Dexter, *Yale Graduates*, 1:380–82.

39. [Joseph Haynes], *The Priests Lips Should Keep Knowledge . . . Articles of charge against the Revd Mr Bacheller . . .* (Portsmouth, N.H.: 1760), 6–50.

40. Thomas Symmes, *An Ordination Sermon preach'd at Malden, Octob. 31, 1721 . . .* (Boston, 1722), 14, 26.

41. *History of Morris County New Jersey* (New York: Munsell, 1882), 198, quoted in Sibley 10:405–416.

42. "Henry Lucas to the Secretary of the S.P.G., July 24, 1716," in Society for the Propagation of the Gospel Manuscripts, A, 11, 403, quoted in Henry K. Beecher and Mark D. Altschule, *Medicine at Harvard: The First Three Hundred Years* (Hanover, N.H.: Univ. Press of New England, 1977), 5.

43. Azariah Mather, *The Gospel Minister Described . . .* (New London, Conn., 1725), 26, as quoted in Bushman, *Puritan to Yankee*, 158. Willis, *Journals of Smith and Deane*, 133–48; Sibley, *Harvard Graduates*, 6:400–410.

44. Estimates for wealth in 1774 can be found in Alice Hanson Jones, *Wealth of a Nation to Be* (New York: Columbia Univ. Press, 1980), 224, table 7.5. Also helpful is Perkins, *Economy of Colonial America*, 152–62. For the 17th century, see Terry L. Anderson, *The Economic Growth of Seventeenth-Century New England: A Measurement of Regional Income* (New York: Arno, 1974), and for the 18th, see Bruce C. Daniels, "Long Range Trends of Wealth Distribution in Eighteenth-Century New England," *Explorations in Economic History* (Winter 1973–74):123–35. A comprehensive economic history of colonial New England is William B. Weeden, *Economic and Social History of New England, 1620–1789* (Boston, 1891), but it is largely antiquarian in approach. A recent and penetrating economic history of the British colonies in the New World is John J. McCusker and Russell R. Menard, *The Economy of British America, 1607–1789* (Chapel Hill: Univ. of North Carolina Press, 1985). The book is conveniently broken down into regional analyses, and the section on New England is very helpful.

45. Bushman, *Puritan to Yankee*, 286–87.

46. Sibley, *Harvard Graduates*, 4:113–17, 381–83. Michael Walzer, "Puritanism as a Revolutionary Ideology," *History and Theory* 3 (1963):66–67.

47. Thomas Symmes, *An Ordination Sermon Preach'd at Malden*, 5.

Chapter 3

1. R.S. Roberts. "The Personnel and Practice of Medicine in Tudor and Stuart England: Part I. The Provinces," *Medical History* 6 (1962):363–82. For a discussion of the lack of professional structure among health practitioners in 17th-century New England, see "Letters of Samuel Lee and Samuel Sewall," 146.

2. For a discussion of the contents of the libraries of Puritan ministers,

see Tuttle, "Libraries of the Mathers," 269, and Samuel Eliot Morison, *The Intellectual Life of Colonial New England* (New York Univ., 1936; rpt. ed. Ithaca, N.Y.: Cornell Univ. Press, 1965), 133–40. Morison claims that his analysis of clerical libraries confirms the "tradition that early New England ministers generally practiced medicine as well as religion," 140.

3. For example, see William Salmon, *Supplement to the London Dispensatory* (London, 1688) and *New London Dispensatory* (London, 1707).

4. Nicholas Culpeper, *A Physical Directory* (London, 1650, 2Ar), as quoted in Webster, *Great Instauration*, 271. The only full-length work on the life and writings of Nicholas Culpeper is Rex Jones, "Genealogy of a Classic: The *English Physitian* of Nicholas Culpeper," Ph.D. diss., Univ. of California, San Francisco, 1984.

5. Franklin B. Dexter, "Early Private Libraries in New England," *Proceedings* of the AAS 18 (1907):136, 143. For lists of booksellers who commonly sold Culpeper's works, see W.C. Ford, *The Boston Book Market, 1670–1700* (Boston, 1917), 84, 99, 109, 131, 146.

6. On the role of women as providers of household medicine in 17th-century England, see Nagy, *Popular Medicine*. David L. Cowen, "The Boston Editions of Nicholas Culpeper," *Journal of the History of Medicine and Allied Sciences* 11 (1956):165. Sibley, *Harvard Graduates*, 3:475. A large majority of the ministers took the master of arts degree three years after the first degree was awarded.

7. Charles Webster, "The Poor Man's Physician," *Great Instauration*, 256–64. Cowen, "Boston Editions," 161.

8. "Culpeper, Nicholas," in *Dictionary of National Biography*, ed. Sir Leslie Stephen and Sir Sydney Lee (New York: Macmillan, 1897), 5:286; Cowen, "Boston Editions," 159–60.

9. Thomas Palmer, *The Admirable Secrets of Physick and Chirurgery*, ed. Thomas R. Forbes (New Haven: Yale Univ. Press, 1985), 36.

10. Nicholas Culpeper, *Pharmacopoeia Londinensis, or the London Dispensatory* (Boston, 1720), introduction. On the intricacies of Galenic theory and therapy, see Lester S. King, *The Road to the Medical Enlightenment, 1650–1695* (London: MacDonald, 1970), 15–23. For a general introduction to Galenic medicine, see Erwin H. Ackerknecht, *A Short History of Medicine*, rev. ed. (Baltimore, Md.: Johns Hopkins Univ. Press, 1982), 53. Although Thomas Palmer considered Paracelsian remedies to be superior to Galenic ones, his "Dispensatory" contains many lengthy passages on Galenic theory and therapies. See Palmer, *Admirable Secrets*, 49–50.

11. Culpeper, *Pharmacopoeia Londinensis*.

12. Ann Leighton, *Early American Gardens: For Meate or Medicine* (Wor-

cester, Mass.: AAS, 1970), 115. Thomas Symmes, Notebook, 1696–1774, AAS.

13. Dexter, *Yale Graduates* 1 (1701–1745):52–56. Peter Tolman to Gershom Bulkeley, 15 July 1698, Gershom Bulkeley Papers, Hartford Medical Society. Ezra Carpenter, [Memory Book], Houghton Library, Harvard University. Comfrey, a healing herb, was known to the ancient Greeks and Romans. The leaves or roots were made into a poultice ("plaister"), which was thought to be beneficial for sprains, swellings, bruises, and the suppression of bleeding. For a description of the healing properties of many of the medicinal herbs used by the colonists, see Francesco Bianchini and Francesco Corbetta, *Health Plants of the World* (New York: Newsweek Books, 1979).

14. Quoted in Walter Steiner, "The Reverend Gershom Bulkeley, of Connecticut, An Eminent Clerical Physician," *Johns Hopkins Hospital Bulletin* 17 (1906):51.

15. Timothy Harris, Notebook, AAS. Also at AAS, see the collection of colonial manuscript cookbooks which often contain medical remedies. For a study of herbal remedies of the New England colonists, see Leighton, *Early American Gardens*.

16. Parkman Family Papers, AAS. For a detailed study of diphtheria epidemics in colonial New England, see Ernest Caulfield, A *True History of the Terrible Epidemic Vulgarly Called the Throat Distemper* (New Haven, Conn.: Beaumont Club, 1939).

17. Gershom Bulkeley Papers, Mss. N.C. Med. Pro. Pauperibus, Hartford Medical Society. Thomas H. Johnson, *The Poetical Works of Edward Taylor* (Princeton, N.J.: Princeton Univ. Press, 1943), 201–220. Herbert, *The Countrey Parson*, 61–62.

18. Palmer, *Admirable Secrets*, 49–50.

19. Michael Wigglesworth, *Meat out of the Eater: Or Afflictions Unto Gods Children* (Cambridge, Mass., 1670), 11. For a listing of the contents of Wigglesworth's library, see "Rev. Michael Wigglesworth, His Memoir, Autobiography, Letters, and Library," NEHGR 17 (1863):142.

20. On the aloe plant, see Bianchini and Corbetta, *Health Plants of the World*, 28. On the procurement of medicinal plants from the West Indies, see Leighton, *Early American Gardens*, 123. Herbert, *The Countrey Parson*, 63. Wigglesworth, *Meat out of the Eater*, 46.

21. Giles Firmin, *Separation Examined* (London, 1652), 45.

22. Donald Sanford, *The Poems of Edward Taylor* (New Haven: Yale Univ. Press, 1960), 11–12.

23. William T. McNeil, *Cure of Souls*, vii–viii, 263–64. Susan Sontag discusses changes in American patterns of medical metaphor over the course of the 19th and 20th centuries in her provocative essay, *Illness as Metaphor* (New York: Vintage, 1979).

24. Michael Wigglesworth, *Meat out of the Eater*, 5th ed. (Boston, 1717), 25. Herbert, *The Countrey Parson*, 45.

25. Charles Chauncy, *The Plain Doctrine of Justification of a Sinner in the Sight of God* . . . (London, 1659), 43.

26. McNeil, *Cure of Souls*, 275–77.

27. `Nicholas Culpeper, *Pharmacopoeia Londinensis*, introduction. William D. Stahlman, "Astrology in Colonial America: An Extended Inquiry," *William and Mary Quarterly* 13 (1956):559. Thomas R. Forbes, "Introduction," in Palmer, *Admirable Secrets*, 13. Cotton Mather, *Angel of Bethesda*, 301.

28. Gershom Bulkeley Papers, Notes on Riverius, Hartford Medical Society. Palmer, *Admirable Secrets*, 15, 45 and editor's note. See table 3.1 in this book for a list of those ministers who owned works by Riverius. For a study of the medical philosophy of Riverius, see King, *Road to the Medical Enlightenment*, 15–37. Whether or not Galen himself believed in the importance of astrology in relation to the critical days was a subject of much debate during the Renaissance. See King, *Road to the Medical Enlightenment*, 29.

29. Taylor's library is in Johnson, *Poetical Works of Edward Taylor*, 201–220. Edward Taylor, Dispensatory, Beineke Rare Book Library, Yale University, 41.

30. Ezra Carpenter, [Memory Book], Houghton Library, Harvard University.

31. The argument from Calvin is from his *Avertissement contre l'astrologie* (1549; Paris: Librarie Armand Colin, 1972), 6, quoted in Wayne Shumaker, *The Occult Sciences in the Renaissance: A Study of Intellectual Patterns* (Berkeley: Univ. of California Press, 1972), 44–48.

32. Letter from John Allin, 8 Nov. 1665, quoted in Cooper, "Notices of the Last Great Plague," 17. Allin's close friend and correspondent, Samuel Jeake, mentioned in the letter, also was an astrologer who was known to have cast over 150 horoscopes. See Alvan Lamson, *Sermon Preached October 31, 1858* (Boston: Crosby, Nichols and Co., 1849), 42. For a biographical sketch of Allin, see Sibley, *Harvard Graduates*, 2:137–38.

33. Nathaniel Ames, Jr., *Almanac for 1729* (Boston, 1729), quoted in Samuel Biggs, *The Essays, Humor and Poems of Nathaniel Ames* (Cleveland, Ohio, 1891), 60. For diagrams of the "Man of Signs," see Elizabeth Carroll Riley, *Dictionary of Colonial America Printers Ornaments* (Worcester, Mass.: AAS, 1975), 443. The Man of Signs or Anatomy is thought to date back to European almanacs of the 12th century. See Robb Sagendorph, *America and her Almanacs* (Dublin, N.H.: 1970), 46. As early as 1506, the English *Kalendar of Shepherdes* warned that "a man ought not to make incysyon [on] . . . ye membre gouerned of any sygne the day that the moone is in it for fere of to grete effusyon of blode that myght happen, ne in lykewyse also when the sonne is in it, for the daunger & peryll that myght ensue." See George Lyman Kittredge, *The Old Farmer and His Almanack* (rpt. ed., Williamstown,

Mass.: Cornerhouse, 1974), 53. For a study of the medical contents in early American almanacs, see Francisco Guerra, "Medical Almanacs of the American Colonial Period," *Journal of the History of Medical and Allied Sciences* 16 (1961):234–55.

34. Rev. Gershom Bulkeley, Interleaved Almanack for 1699, Library of Congress, Manuscript Division. Gershom Bulkeley Papers, Document no. 11, Hartford Medical Society.

35. Harold S. Jantz, "Christian Lodowick of Newport and Leipzig," *Rhode Island History* 3 (1944):108, 4 (1945):13–15.

36. Christian Lodowick, *The New-England Almanack for the Year . . . 1695* (Boston, 1695), 15–16. On the popularity of the "Man of Signs" among lay readers of New England almanacs, see S. Biggs, *Essays*, 58–61. Almanac makers, bowing to public pressure, continued to include the "Man of Signs" through the 19th century. Increase Mather, *Kometographia* (Boston, 1683), 130. The example of Thomas Erastus is from Shumaker, *Occult Sciences*, 47.

37. P.I.H. Naylor, *Astrology: An Historical Examination* (Hollywood: Wilshire Book Co., 1974), 97. Webster, *Great Instauration*, 5.

38. Marie Boas, *The Scientific Renaissance: 1450–1630* (New York: Harper and Row), 171, and Webster, *Great Instauration*, 5.

39. Jon Butler, "Magic, Astrology, and the Early American Religious Heritage, 1600–1760," *American Historical Review* 84 (1979):337;341. Herbert Leventhal, *In the Shadow of the Enlightenment: Occultism and Renaissance Science in Eighteenth-Century America* (New York: New York Univ. Press, 1976), 19, 29, 64–65. The continued acceptance of astrology among the masses in England is documented in Naylor, *Astrology*, 113–16.

40. See table 3.1. Cotton Mather, *Angel of Bethesda*, 262, 68, 249.

41. Richard D. Brown, "Spreading the Word: Rural Clergymen and the Communication Network of 18th-Century New England," *Proceedings* of the AAS 94 (1982):1–14.

Chapter 4

1. Palmer, *Admirable Secrets*, 167. For a list of the authors consulted by Palmer in the preparation of his dispensatory, see Thomas R. Forbes, "Introduction," in Palmer, *Admirable Secrets*, 15.

2. Charles Webster, "Alchemical and Paracelsian Medicine," in Webster, *Health, Medicine and Mortality*, 312–15. For a detailed study of the medical reform movement during the Puritan Revolution in England, see Webster, *Great Instauration*. The intricacies of Paracelsian medicine are explored in Walter Pagel, *Paracelsus: An Introduction to Philosophical Medicine in the Era of the Renaissance* (New York: S. Karger, 1958).

3. Fielding H. Garrison, *An Introduction to the History of Medicine*, 4th ed. (Philadelphia: W.B. Saunders, 1929), 205; Webster, *Great Instauration*, 286.

4. John Woodall, *The Surgions Mate* (London, 1639), 309f., quoted in Allen G. Debus, "John Woodall, Paracelsian Surgeon," *Ambix* 10 (1962), 113.

5. Woodall, *The Surgions Mate* (London, 1617), quoted in Debus, "John Woodall," 116.

6. Owen Hannaway, *The Chemists and the Word: The Didactic Origins of Chemistry* (Baltimore, Md.: Johns Hopkins Univ. Press, 1975), 38–43.

7. Webster, *Great Instauration*, 284–85.

8. This quotation is from the English translation of Oswald Croll, "Admonitory Preface" to his *Basilica Chymica*, in Croll, *Philosophy Reformed and Improved in Four Profound Tractates. The I. Discovering the Great and Deep Mysteries of Nature: By that Learned Chymist and Physitian Osw: Crollius*, trans. H. Pinnell (London, 1657), 93, quoted in Hannaway, *The Chemists*, 43. Webster, "Alchemical and Paracelsian Medicine," 315; Palmer, *Admirable Secrets*, 165–68.

9. Martin Luther, *Table Talk*, 805, quoted in Stanton J. Linden, "Alchemy and Eschatology in Seventeenth-Century Poetry," *Ambix* 31 (1984):103.

10. Linden, "Alchemy and Eschatology," 103.

11. Croll, "Admonitory Preface," 190–91, quoted in Hannaway, *The Chemists*, 51. Also see Hannaway, *The Chemists*, 47–56.

12. Gerald Schroder, "Oswald Crollius," in *Dictionary of Scientific Biography*, ed. Charles Gillespie (New York: Scribner's, 1975), 3:471–72. Sir Thomas Browne, *Selected Writings*, ed. by Sir Geoffrey Keynes (Chicago: Univ. of Chicago Press, 1968), 413–14.

13. Jean Calvin, *Institutes of the Christian Religion*, ed. John T. McNeil, tr. Ford Lewis Battles (Philadelphia: Westminster Press, 1960), 1:292–93 (bk. II, ch. iii, sec. 3).

14. "Bloomfields Blossoms: or, The Campe of Philosophy," in *Theatrum Chemicum Britannicum*, comp. by Elias Ashmole (London, 1952; facsimile rpt., New York: Johnson Reprint Corp., 1967), 307, quoted in Robert Schuler, "William Blomfild, Elizabethan Alchemist," *Ambix* 20 (1973):85. For a more detailed explanation of the parallels between alchemy and various strains of Protestantism in 17th-century England, see Robert M. Schuler, "Some Spiritual Alchemies of Seventeen-Century England," *Journal of the History of Ideas* 41 (1980):304–306.

15. Linden, "Alchemy and Eschatology," 102–124. Also see his "Alchemy and the English Literary Imagination: 1385–1633," Ph.D. diss., Univ. of Minnesota, 1971).

16. Michael Wigglesworth, *Meat Out of the Eater*, 5th ed. (Boston, 1717), 46. "Rev. Michael Wigglesworth, His Memoir, Autobiography, Letters, and Library," NEHGR 17 (1863):142.

17. The verse is from a poem by Anne Bradstreet, quoted by Perry Miller, *The New England Mind: The Seventeenth Century*, 2d ed. Cambridge, Mass.: Harvard Univ. Press, 1954), 361–62. Edward Taylor, "Meditation 4, I am the Rose of Sharon," written in Apr. 1683, in Donald Sanford, *The Poems of Edward Taylor*, 2d ed. (New Haven, Conn.: Yale Univ. Press, 1963), 13.

18. Edward Taylor, "Meditation 7, Grace in thy lips poured out," written in Feb. 1683, in Sanford, *Poems of Edward Taylor*, 17.

19. Herbert, *The Countrey Parson*, 59, 123–24.

20. Edward Taylor, "Meditation 49, Full of Grace," written in Nov. 1702, in Sanford, *Poems of Edward Taylor*, 165.

21. Edward Taylor, "Meditation 9, I am the Living Bread," written in Sept. 1684, in Sanford, *Poems of Edward Taylor*, 19–20. On the use of alchemical metaphor in Taylor's poetry, see Cheryl Z. Orevicz, "Edward Taylor and the Alchemy of Grace," *Seventeenth-Century News* (1976), 33, 34.

22. F.N.L. Poynter, "Nicholas Culpeper and the Paracelsians," in Allen G. Debus, ed., *Science, Medicine and Society in the Renaissance*, 2 vols. (New York: Science History Publications, 1972), 1:212.

23. Sir Thomas Browne, *Pseudodoxia Epidemica* (London, 1646), bk. I, ch. 7, quoted in Charles Webster, "English Medical Reformers of the Puritan Revolution: A Background to the 'Society of Chemical Physitians,'" *Ambix* 14 (1967):28.

24. Cooper, "Notices of the Last Great Plague," 2–9.

25. Morgan, "Diary of Rev. Michael Wigglesworth," 325. Urian Oakes, *The Soveraign of Divine Providence*, quoted by Miller, *New England Mind: Colony to Province*, 349. *Letters of John Davenport*, 183, quoted in Geddes, *Welcome Joy*, 43. Geddes's chapter entitled "Harbingers of Death" in this volume provides an interesting analysis of Puritan perceptions of illness in New England.

26. Edward Taylor Manuscripts, Beineke Rare Book Library, Yale Univ., New Haven, Conn. Taylor's estate inventory is at the Probate Record Office, Northhampton, Mass., taken 29 Aug. 1729. For a published list of the contents of his library, see Karl Keller, *The Example of Edward Taylor* (Amherst: Univ. of Massachusetts Press, 1975), 295.

27. Ronald S. Wilkinson, "George Starkey, Physician and Alchemist," *Ambix* 11 (1963):121–52. Also see George H. Trumbull, "George Stirk, 'Philosopher by Fire,'" *Publications* of the Colonial Society of Massachusetts 38 (1949):219–51. See J. Worth Estes, "Starkey's Pill," *Journal of the History of Medicine and Allied Sciences* 34 (1970):200.

28. I. Bernard Cohen, "The Beginning of Chemical Instruction in America: A Brief Account of the Teaching of Chemistry at Harvard Prior to 1800," *Chymia* 3 (1950):18. See the biographical sketch of Leonard Hoar in Sibley, *Harvard Graduates*, 1:228–52.

29. Fairfield County Probate Files, 1703. Isaac Chauncy to Gershom

Bulkeley, 26 May 1699 and 4 Apr. 1695, Gershom Bulkeley Papers, Hartford Medical Society.

30. Samuel E. Morison, *Harvard College in the Seventeenth Century* (Cambridge, Mass.: Harvard Univ. Press, 1936), 129–32; Cohen, "Beginning of Chemical Instruction," 19–21.

31. ˙Cohen, "Beginning of Chemical Instruction," 19–21.

32. Ronald S. Wilkinson, "New England's Last Alchemists," *Ambix* 10 (1962):128–29; Brock, "Influence of Europe on Colonial Massachusetts Medicine," 104; Cohen, "Beginning of Chemical Instruction," 21–33, 34–35. Charles Morton, *Compendium Physicae,* ed. Samuel Eliot Morison *Publications* of the Colonial Society of Massachusetts 33 (1940). In Morison's *Harvard College in the Seventeenth Century,* he discusses an increase in the numbers of "modern" theses which dealt with the physical sciences after the introduction of Morton's work, 129–32.

33. Cotton Mather, *Magnalia* (1853), i, 602, quoted in "Samuel Lee," *Dictionary of National Biography,* ed. Sir Leslie Stephen and Sir Sidney Lee (London: Oxford Univ. Press, 1917), 11:818.

34. Thomas Prince's "Preface" to Nathaniel Williams, *The Method of Practice in the Small Pox, With Observations on the Way of Inoculation* (Boston, 1752), quoted in Jantz, "Christian Lodowick," 4:13. Morgan, "Diary of Michael Wigglesworth," 404–405.

35. Samuel Lee to Nehemiah Grew, M.D. (1641–1712), 1691, in "Letters of Samuel Lee and Samuel Sewall," 147.

36. Jantz, "Christian Lodowick," 3:108; 4:13–15.

37. See Webster, *Great Instauration.*

38. MacDonald, *Mystical Bedlam,* 32; Sir George Clark, A *History of the Royal College of Physicians of London* (Oxford, England: Clarendon Press, 1966), I, 246–47. Also see Harold J. Cook, "The Regulation of Medical Practice in London under the Stuarts, 1607–1704," (Ph.D. diss., Univ. of Michigan, Ann Arbor, 1981), 194.

39. Perry Miller, *New England Mind: Colony to Province,* 345. For a list of the handful of physicians with European medical degrees who practiced in colonial New England before the arrival of Douglas, see C.Helen Brock and Eric H. Christianson, "A Biographical Register of Men and Women from and Immigrants to Massachusetts between 1620 and 1800 Who Received Some Medical Training in Europe," in Cash, Christianson, and Estes, *Medicine in Colonial Massachusetts,* [117–43]. On Lodowick's training, see Jantz, "Christian Lodowick," 3:107.

40. Thomas Hall, *Histrio-Mastix* (London, 1654), 199, quoted in Schuler, "Some Spiritual Alchemies," 303. Schuler has argued that Englishmen of varying religious backgrounds in the first half of the 17th century, including moderate Anglicans, orthodox Calvinists, and radical Puritans, "could find

in alchemy something to harmonize with their very different religious beliefs and experience," 294. See also Linden, who in "Alchemy and Eschatology," 120, agrees with Schuler on the widespread appeal of alchemy to various Protestant strains. For Keith Thomas's views on the links between Hermeticism and the radical Puritan sects during the Civil War period, see his *Religion and the Decline of Magic*, 227. Also see Christopher Hill, "The Medical Profession and its Radical Critics," in Christopher Hill, *Change and Continuity in Seventeenth Century England*, (Cambridge, Mass.: Harvard Univ. Press, 1975), 157–78; Hill, *Intellectual Origins of the English Revolution* (Oxford, England: Clarendon Press, 1965), 147–48; 298; and Hill, *Milton and the English Revolution* (New York: Viking 1978), 76. In the last, Hill claims that during the 1640s and 1650s "not all Hermeticists were radicals, by a long way; but most radicals were Hermeticists."

41. P.M. Rattansi, "Paracelsus and the Puritan Revolution," *Ambix* 11 (1963): 24–32; Webster, "English Medical Reformers," 16–41.

42. A listing of the earliest donations to the young college can be found in Andrew McFarland Davis, "A Few Notes Concerning the Records of Harvard College," *Bibliographical Contributions of Harvard University*, no. 27 (1888), pp. 6–7. Harvard's earliest benefactor and namesake, John Harvard, donated a work by Levinus Lemnius, *The Touchstone of Complexions . . .*, which was quite popular in northern Germany through the first third of the 17th century. This volume dealt with sympathetic and astrological medicine. The contents of the library in 1723 can be found in *Catalogus Librorum Bibliothecae Collegij Harvardini Quod Est Cantabrigiae in Nova Anglia* (Boston, 1723). An analysis of the holdings reveals the presence of 20 occult volumes, many of them standard works on the natural magic tradition. The occult and other medical volumes taken by Increase Mather from Leonard Hoar's library are itemized in Tuttle, "The Libraries of the Mathers," 291–92.

43. Frances A. Yates, *The Occult Philosophy in the Elizabethan Age* (London: Routledge & Kegan Paul, 1979), 177–81.

44. Ibid., 82.

45. Cotton Mather, *Angel of Bethesda*, 48–49. Two excellent studies of the healing practices of Napier are MacDonald's *Mystical Bedlam* and Sawyer, "Patients, Healers, and Disease." A colonial Anglican churchman by the name of Thomas Teackle who lived in 17th-century Virginia collected an extensive occult library, underscoring the contention that medical occultism among the clergy was by no means strictly a Puritan phenomenon. See Jon Butler, "Magic, Astrology and the Early American Religious Heritage," 326–30. Also see Leventhal, *In the Shadow of the Enlightenment*.

46. See Avihu Zakai, "Exile and Kingdom: Reformation, Separation, and the Millenial Quest in the Formation of Massachusetts and Its Relationship

with England, 1628–1660" (Ph.D. diss., Johns Hopkins Univ., 1983), which explores the presence of radical thought in Puritan New England.

47. Shumaker, *Occult Sciences*, 113–14.

48. Palmer, *Admirable Secrets*, 20.

49. Walter B. Steiner, "The Reverend Gershom Bulkeley," 48–53; Bulkeley Family Papers, AAS.

50. "The Winthrop Papers," Collection of the Massachusetts Historical Society, 6th ser., 5 (1892):302.

51. Hartford County (Conn.) Probate Files, 1738, and Middletown County (Conn.) Probate Files, 1767.

52. Wilkinson, "New England's Last Alchemists," 133. Ezra Stiles's diary for 2 Mar. 1789 records, "This afternoon Dr. ——— visited me to discourse on Chemistry and inquiring concerning the hermetic Philosophy," and for 3 March, "Dr. ——— visited me again to-day to converse about the Transmutation of metals, which he says Dr. Koon performed at Wallingford last December. He is infatuated with the notion that I know something about it. I told him that I knew nothing but what is in the books; that I never possessed the secret, if there was any . . . that I had never performed transmutation nor seen it performed, and that I held the whole thing to be a vain and illusory pursuit." Quoted in Henry Bronson, "Medical History and Biography," *Papers of the New Haven Colony Historical Society*, 2:263.

Jon Butler discusses the waning of certain forms of occultism in the colonies in "Magic, Astrology and the Early American Religious Heritage," 326–30. Although Butler's article is one of the most thorough treatments of the influence of occultism on early American medicine, his chronology for the waxing and waning of specific occult influences is problematical because of a lack of well-documented evidence to support his claims.

53. Allen G. Debus, "The Paracelsians in Eighteenth Century France: A Renaissance Tradition in the Age of the Enlightenment," *Ambix* 28 (1981): 36–54.

54. Herman Boerhaave, *A New Method of Chemistry* . . ., trans. Peter Shaw, 2 vols., 2d ed. (London, 1741), 1:65; quoted in Hannaway, *The Chemists*, 155.

55. G.H. Turnbull, ed., "Some Correspondence of John Winthrop, Jr., and Samuel Hartlib," *Proceedings* of the Massachusetts Historical Society 72 (1957–60): 36–41; 50–51.

56. Cotton Mather, *Magnalia*, bk. III, p. 223. For more on Winthrop, see Robert C. Black, *The Younger John Winthrop* (New York: Columbia Univ. Press, 1966). A list of the contents of the Bulkeley library is in the Bulkeley Family Papers, AAS. For a list of works in the library of Samuel Lee, see Duncan Campbell, *The Library of the Late Reverend & Learned Mr. Samuel Lee* (Boston, 1693). For a biographical sketch of Lee, see Stephen and Lee, *Dic-*

tionary of National Biography, vol. 11. On Winthrop's collection, see Ronald S. Wilkinson, "The Alchemical Library of John Winthrop, Jr., and His Descendants in Colonial America," *Ambix* 11 (1963):33–51; and 13 (1965):133–86. Quote on 11:50.

57. Ronald S. Wilkinson, "'Hermes Christianus:' John Winthrop, Jr., and Chemical Medicine in Seventeenth-Century New England," in Allen G. Debus, ed., *Science, Medicine and Society in the Renaissance* (New York: Science History Publications, 1972), 237, n. 10.

58. On colonial replication of English society, see Jack P. Greene, "Search for Identity: An Interpretation of the Meaning of Selected Patterns of Social Response in Eighteenth-Century America," *Journal of Social History* 6 (1970):189; and Jack P. Greene and J.R. Pole, "Reconstructing British-American Colonial History: An Introduction," in Jack P. Greene and J.R. Pole, eds. *Colonial British America: Essays in the New History of the Early Modern Era* (Baltimore, Md.: Johns Hopkins Univ. Press, 1984), 1–17. Also see J.P. Greene, *Pursuits of Happiness: The Social Development of Early Modern British Colonies and the Formation of American Culture* (Chapel Hill: Univ. of North Carolina Press, 1988).

59. Arthur O. Norton, "Harvard Textbooks and Reference Books of the Seventeenth-Century," *Publications* of the Colonial Society of Massachusetts 28 (1930–33): 402–406.

60. Charles Webster, *From Paracelsus to Newton: Magic and the Making of Modern Science* (Cambridge, England: Cambridge Univ. Press, 1983), 65.

61. Gershom Bulkeley Papers, Hartford Medical Society.

62. J. Worth Estes, personal communication ca. Nov. 1989.

Chapter 5

1. Dexter, *Yale Graduates,* 1:151–54.

2. For bookdealers who stocked surgical texts, see Morison, *Intellectual Life of Colonial New England,* 130. A list of the medical and surgical authorities consulted by Thomas Palmer is in the introduction to Palmer, *Admirable Secrets,* 15.

3. Royal College of Physicians, *Annals,* 1608–47, p. 156, quoted in R.S. Roberts, "The Personnel and Practice of Medicine in Tudor and Stuart England. Part II: London," *Medical History* 6 (1962):226. Debus also points out that the surgeons of Tudor England were the first body of practitioners to adopt the new mineral and chemical remedies of the Paracelsians on a widespread basis, but he also points out that many members of the Royal College of Physicians favored Paracelsian remedies. See his "John Woodall," 108.

4. G. Parker, *The Early History of Surgery in Great Britain* (London: A. & C. Black, 1920), 111–13.

5. Palmer, *Admirable Secrets*, 74–76, 81, 123–24. William C. Wigglesworth, "Surgery in Massachusetts, 1620–1800," in Cash, Christianson, and Estes, *Medicine in Colonial Massachusetts*, 216–17. For the types of surgical practice performed by colonial physicians as part of their general practice, see J. Worth Estes, "Therapeutic Practice in Colonial New England," in Cash, Christianson, and Estes, *Medicine in Colonial Massachusetts*, [300–301], 303–305.

6. Gordon H. Jones, "Introduction" to Cotton Mather, *Angel of Bethesda*, xxviii; James Cooke, *The Marrow of Chirurgery* (London, 1648), 264.

7. Palmer, *Admirable Secrets*, 89–90.

8. Parkman Family Papers, AAS. Francis G. Walett, ed., *The Diary of Ebenezer Parkman, 1703–1782* (Worcester, Mass.: AAS, 1974), 253–55.

9. Cotton Mather, *Angel of Bethesda*, 247.

10. Zerobabel Endecott, *Synopsis Medicinae or A Compendium of Galenical and Chymical Physick* . . . , ed. George Francis Dow (Salem, Mass.: Essex Tracts, no. 9, 1914), 26, 21.

11. Eli Forbes's account of the treatment is in the Edward Holyoke Manuscripts, Essex Institute, 2:116–17; and 2:119, quoted in Clifford K. Shipton, *Biographical Sketches of Those Who Attended Harvard College* (Boston: Massachusetts Historical Society, 1942) 13:47. Cotton Mather reputedly greatly feared cancer, and it is thought that his first wife died of breast cancer. See Cotton Mather, *Angel of Bethesda*, xxxii.

12. Cotton Mather, *Angel of Bethesda*, xxviii; 82–87. Rev. Samuel Wigglesworth, Account Book c. 1714–c. 1768, NEHGS. John Duffy, personal communication, 8 June 1988.

13. Amundsen, "Medieval Canon Law," 39, 22–44.

14. Ibid., 22–44.

15. For an interpretation of the role of Puritanism in maintaining social stability in 17th-century New England, see Breen and Foster, "The Puritans' Greatest Achievement," 5–22. On other reasons that ministers or regular physicians may have been reluctant to engage in surgery, see Estes, "Therapeutic Practice," 289–363.

16. Gershom Bulkeley, Sermon Notes, 1661–62, Gershom Bulkeley Papers, Hartford Medical Society. Sibley, *Harvard Graduates*, 2:390–93. Bulkeley's library holdings are listed in the Bulkeley Family Papers, AAS. Steiner, "Reverend Gershom Bulkeley," 48–53. On the scarcity of surgeons before 1740, see Eric H. Christianson, "Individuals in the Healing Arts and the Emergence of a Medical Community in Massachusetts: 1700–1792" (Ph.D. diss., Univ. of Southern California, Los Angeles, 1976), 112.

17. Sibley, *Harvard Graduates*, 2:84–87; 3:364–66.

18. Christianson, "Individuals in the Healing Arts," 111–12. Brock and Christianson, "A Biographical Register," pp. [117–43], lists 23 surgeons who practiced before 1740.

19. John Graham, *Extracts from the Journal of the Reverend John Graham, Chaplain of the First Connecticut Regiment, Colonel Lyman, From September 25th to October 18th, 1762, at the Siege of Havana* (New York: Society of Colonial Wars, 1896), 5–11; Dexter, *Yale Graduates*, 1:648–49.

20. Sanford, *Edward Taylor*, 39. For an interesting study of attitudes toward death and dying in Puritan New England, see Geddes, *Welcome Joy*.

21. Sibley, *Harvard Graduates*, 8:692–95. Also see the biographical sketch of Rev. Jonathan Pierpont (1695–1758), another army chaplain and surgeon, in ibid., 6:69–71.

22. Ibid., 7:502–509.

23. Ibid., 11:216–17. John Crocker (HC 1743) also tried his hand at preaching and, failing to obtain a settlement, practiced medicine and then joined the Revolutionary Army as surgeon in 1775; ibid., 16:325–36. Eric H. Christianson found that, in 1741–1785, 231 men served as surgeons or surgeons' mates at sea, on the battlefields, and in hospitals. Before 1740, only a handful of men acted in a surgical capacity in the military. See Christianson, "Individuals in the Healing Arts," 111–12. For more detail on the military as a stimulus to surgical and medical practice, see Philip Cash, *Medical Men at the Siege of Boston, April 1755–April 1776* (Philadelphia: American Philosophical Society, 1939); William C. Owen, ed., *The Medical Department of the U.S. Army During the Period of the Revolution* (New York: Hieber, 1920); Walter Steiner, "Dr. James Thacher of Plymouth, An Erudite Physician of Revolutionary and Post-Revolutionary Fame," *Bulletin of the History of Medicine* 1 (1933):157–73.

24. Samuel Brackenbury's library is listed in the manuscript, Suffolk County (Mass.) Probate Files, Boston, 12:207–208, 1677–78. "Bartholin, Thomas," in Gillespie, *Dictionary of Scientific Biography*, 1:482–83.

25. "Willis, Thomas," in Gillespie, *Dictionary of Scientific Biography*, 14:404–409; Garrison, *Introduction to the History of Medicine*, 262–64. Also see Robert G. Frank, Jr., *Harvey and the Oxford Physiologists* (Berkeley: Univ. of California Press, 1980).

26. "Riolan, Jean," in Gillespie, *Dictionary of Scientific Biography*, 11:466–68. *Catalogus Librorum Bibliothecae Collegij Harvardini Quod est Cantabrigiae in Nova Anglia* (Boston: Printed by B. Green. 1723) and *A Catalogue of the Library of Yale College in New Haven* (New London: Printed by T. Green, 1743).

27. Richard H. Shryock, *Medicine and Society in America, 1660–1860* (Ithaca, N.Y.: Cornell Univ. Press, 1960), 47. For a listing of Wigglesworth's library, see "Rev. Michael Wigglesworth, His Memoir, Autobiography, Letters and Library," NEHGR 17 (1863):142. For Lee's library, see *The Library of the Late Reverend and Learned Mr. Samuel Lee* (Boston: Printed for Duncan Campbell, 1693; rptd. 1921). For a biographical sketch of Rowland Cotton, see Sibley, *Harvard Graduates*, 3:290–93.

28. Katharine Park, *Doctors and Medicine in Early Renaissance Florence* (Princeton, N.J.: Princeton Univ. Press, 1985), 53.

29. Pope, "*Notebook of John Fiske*," 49–50. The editor has suggested that the infant's death may have been due to an accidental craniotomy.

30. Sibley, *Harvard Graduates*, 9:12. Hugh Adams (HC 1697) also delivered a parishioner of a baby. He prefaced the procedure with prayer, quoting I Tim. 2:15, which says that "the woman shall be saved in child bearing." Adams then administered "strong Hysterick medicines" to speed up the labor process, and dilated her with "Unguentum Aperitivum meipsum." A problem arose in the delivery, as Adams realized that the baby was in a "most unusual and improbable posture"; he therefore prayed to God for assistance and found that the infant moved to a "capable position." After the delivery, Adams baptized the infant for fear that it would not live long. See Hugh Adams, Manuscript Autobiographical Narrative, Belknap Papers, Massachusetts Historical Society, 28–29.

A midwife's reputation also was on the line during every birth at which she assisted. Alice Tilly, a midwife on board Winthrop's ship *Arabella,* was accused of the "miscarrying of many wimen and children under hir hand" during the 1630s in Boston, but the women of the town rallied to her support. See Darrett B. Rutman, *Winthrop's Boston*, 136, 231.

31. Gordon H. Jones, "Medical and Scientific Books in Colonial Virginia," *Bulletin of the History of Medicine* 40 (1966):156–57. Treatises on midwifery, such as Nicholas Culpeper's *The Complete Midwife's Practice Enlarged* (London, 1680), were owned by Rev. Gershom Bulkeley, who was a surgeon. Also popular among ministers in the middle decades of the 18th century was the work *Midwifery* by the famous author William Smellie (1697–1763), who has been credited with raising the midwife's art to a science. See Garrison, *Introduction to the History of Medicine*, 338.

32. Endecott, *Synopsis Medicinae*, 7; "Letters of Samuel Lee and Samuel Sewall," 14:147.

33. [John Winthrop], *A Short Story of the Rise, Reign, and Ruin of Antinomians, Familists, & Libertines that infected the Churches of New England . . .* (London, 1644), 42–45.

34. Charles J. Hoadly, "Some Early Post-Mortem Examinations in New England," *Proceedings* of the Connecticut Medical Society (1892), 216.

35. Cooper, "Notices of the Last Great Plague," 2.

36. Samuel A. Green, A *History of Medicine in Massachusetts* (Boston: A. Williams, 1881), 257.

37. J. Worth Estes, personal communication, ca. Sept. 1989. Cotton Mather, *Angel of Bethesda*, xxxv; 67; Cotton Mather, *Diary*, 1:65, 1:163–64, quoted in Albert Matthews, "Notes on Early Autopsies and Anatomical Lectures," *Publications* of the Colonial Society of Massachusetts (1917), 19:277.

In 1716, Mather reported the case of a "good man" who was urged to undergo the operation for the cutting of the stone, but he refused to do so and died shortly thereafter. The post-mortem revealed no kidney stone, but rather that "his Bladder was grown entirely schirrous." Quoted in George Lyman Kittredge, "Cotton Mather's Scientific Communications to the Royal Society," *Proceedings* of the AAS 26 (1916):40–41.

38. William Frederick Norwood, "Medical Education in the United States Before 1900," in Charles D. O'Malley, ed., *The History of Medical Education* (Berkeley: Univ. of California Press, 1970), 466.

39. Sibley, *Harvard Graduates*, 1:93.

40. Viets, *Brief History of Medicine in Massachusetts*, 36.

41. Massachusetts Colony Records, 2:201, quoted in Mathews, "Notes on Early Autopsies," 276.

42. Samuel Sewall, *The Diary of Samuel Sewall, 1674–1729*, ed. M. Halsey Thomas, 2 vols. (New York: Farrar, Straus and Giroux, 1973), 1:22–23.

43. Sibley, *Harvard Graduates*, 13:15–16; for a sketch of Stillman's life, see 14:216–27. For Stillman's side of the story, see Samuel Stillman, *Two Sermons, the first . . . Delivered the Lords Day before the Execution of Levi Ames . . .* (Boston, 1773). On the early history of the Boston Medical Society, see Christianson, "Medical Practitioners of Massachusetts," 52n.

44. Philip Cash, "The Professionalization of Boston Medicine, 1760–1803," in Cash, Christianson, and Estes, *Medicine in Colonial Massachusetts*, 76–79. Also see Frederick C. Waite, "The Development of Anatomical Laws in the States of New England," *New England Journal of Medicine* 233 (1945):716–25. On the mimetic impulses of the colonists, see Jack P. Greene, "Search for Identity," 189, and Greene and Pole, "Reconstructing British-American Colonial History," 1–17. Also see Greene's recent work, *Pursuits of Happiness.*

45. David E. Stannard, *The Puritan Way of Death*, 155–63.

46. Cash, "Professionalization of Boston Medicine."

Epilogue

1. Samuel Wigglesworth, *The Blessedness of Such as trust in Christ . . .* (Boston, 1755), 7.

2. See the biography of Thomas Robie in Sibley, *Harvard Graduates*, 5:450–55. The quote is from Miller, *New England Mind: Colony to Province*, 444.

3. Christianson, "Individuals in the Healing Arts," 129.

4. Ibid., 204.

5. Duffy, *The Healers*, 40.

6. Henry D. Rack, "Early Methodist Healing," in Shiels, *The Church and Healing*, 139–52.

7. Examples of contemporary scholarship on religion and medicine include the essays in Shiels, *The Church and Healing*; those in Numbers and Amundsen, *Caring and Curing*; and those in Marty and Vaux, *Health/Medicine*. On the role of midwives in New England, see Laurel Thacher Ulrich's *A Midwife's Tale* (New York: Knopf, 1990). For recent scholarship on colonial British America, see Jack P. Greene, *Pursuits of Happiness*.

Bibliographical Essay

The selection of minister-physicians for this study was based primarily upon three major biographical histories: (1) John Langdon Sibley, ed., *Biographical Sketches of the Graduates of Harvard University*, 17 vols. (Cambridge, Mass.: Charles William Sever, 1873–1975); (2) Franklin B. Dexter, *Biographical Sketches of the Graduates of Yale College: With Annals of College History*, 6 vols. (New York: Holt, 1885–1912); and (3) William Sprague, *Annals of the American Pulpit*, 9 vols. (New York: R. Carter and Bros., 1859–[73]).

In exploring the manuscript and published records of the 126 clergymen in this study, various sources were examined. These include the Probate Records for Suffolk and Middlesex Counties in Massachusetts and for Hartford, New Haven, Sharon, Fairfield, Middletown, Stonginton, and Farmington Counties in Connecticut. Thirty-three percent of the probate inventories of the minister-physicians in this study were located, revealing the itemized contents of nineteen of their libraries, as well as the amount of estate at death for thirty-eight individuals (or 30 percent of the total group). Table 3.1 is based primarily on the book lists in these inventories, as well as on available published library lists of such individuals as Michael Wigglesworth ("Rev. Michael Wigglesworth, His Memoir, Autobiography, Letters, and Library," NEHGR 17 [1863]:142) and Samuel Lee (Duncan Campbell, *The Library of the Late Reverend & Learned Mr. Samuel Lee* [Boston, 1693]). Published diaries were also consulted, including Francis G. Walett, *The Diary of Ebenezer Parkman, 1703–1782* (Worcester, Mass.: American Antiquarian Society, 1974), and Robert G. Pope, *The Notebook of the Reverend John Fiske, 1644–1675* (Boston: *Publications* of the Colonial Society of Massachusetts, 1974). For the study of the minister-physician's use of medical metaphor, the published sermons in the collection of the John Carter Brown Library at Brown University, Providence, Rhode Island, were examined.

The study of the minister-physicians' medical theories and remedies was based largely on the manuscript collections of the American Antiquarian Society; the Hartford Medical Society; the Bulkeley Papers at Trinity College in Hartford, Connecticut; the Beineke Rare Book Library at Yale University; the Houghton Library at Harvard University; the Massachusetts Historical

Society; and the New England Historic and Genealogical Society. Available published *vade mecums* and medical treatises of the ministers in this study were also drawn upon, including Thomas Palmer's *The Admirable Secrets of Physick and Chirurgery*, ed. Thomas R. Forbes (New Haven, Conn.: Yale Univ. Press, 1985), and Cotton Mather's *The Angel of Bethesda*, ed. Gordon H. Jones (Worcester, Mass.: AAS, 1972).

Index